R[illegible]ood:

A [illegible] Times

An exhibition devised by David Blamires

Who Was Robin Hood? What the Early Ballads and Chronicles Tell Us

The first thing that people usually want to know about Robin Hood is: Was he a real person? And if so, when did he live? These are questions asked of many heroes who have entered the popular imagination. What about King Arthur? What about William Tell? What about Siegfried, who won the treasure of the Nibelungs and who, despite his near-invulnerable horny skin, was treacherously murdered in the forest near the River Rhine? For centuries scholars have turned over the literary and historical sources in pursuit of the origins of these heroes, but the end result is speculation rather than certainty.

What are important are the stories told about the heroes. The medieval German poet Hartmann von Aue, writing about the year 1200, says he would not have wanted to live in Arthur's time because it would have meant that he would not be enjoying the tales now. The emphasis is on present delight in the stories, yet there is always a belief that the heroes were men of flesh and blood, that they did actually live, even if the details are not known with certainty. The same is true of Robin Hood. He is first and foremost the hero of certain well-known stories, not a figure of history.

Chaucer's yeoman: woodcut later used as a portrait of Robin Hood *(from item 6)*.

Robin Hood emerges from the shadows of the late Middle Ages first of all as a name. He is first mentioned around 1377 by William Langland in *Piers Plowman* as the subject of 'rymes' that were popular among ordinary people. He was not part of the literature of the aristocracy or the educated classes. Indeed, most of the early allusions to him are disparaging remarks from clerics and the upper classes. Those with power and education have almost always deplored the likes and dislikes and entertainments of those without. Such comments proliferate during the fifteenth and sixteenth centuries. In addition we find proverbs and sayings quoted that mention Robin Hood and, more importantly, we find plays. From 1426-27, when the first play with Robin Hood is documented in Exeter, until nearly the end of the sixteenth century, we have evidence of Robin Hood plays, usually associated with May games, the length and breadth of England and Scotland. Only a few rudimentary texts of these early plays have survived. They generally

Robin, disguised as an old woman, meets the Bishop *(from item 11).*

present a dramatic conflict between Robin and an opponent and can be related to some of the encounters known better from the ballads, but it is not clear whether the plays form the basis of, or derive from, the ballads or whether both represent independent realizations of the same material.

The plays include figures such as Little John and Friar Tuck, and Marian seems to have been linked with them through plays in which Robin appears as a lover rather than an outlaw. The French play *Robin et Marion* by Adam de la Halle provides an example of this, but can hardly be regarded as a direct source. The plays, with their greater similarity to the traditional mummers' play than anything else, seem to belong to the merry-making indulged in at Whitsuntide. They were fundraising events when men from one locality visited another with their performances, and sometimes they got out of hand. By the end of the sixteenth century they appear to have been stopped by pressures from both secular and religious authorities.

Tantalizing as the plays are, it is the early ballads that have placed the most enduring mark of the traditions of Robin Hood. The earliest tangible evidence comes not quite a century after Langland's glancing allusion. Only two ballads have survived in manuscript – *Robin Hood and the Monk* (*c.* 1450) and *Robin Hood and the Potter* (*c.* 1500), both now in Cambridge University Library. Each ballad deals with a single episode. Most significant, however, is the much longer and structurally more complex *Gest of Robin Hood*, which is known with slightly varying titles in five different editions from possibly as early as 1492 up to *c.* 1560. None of these printed texts can be dated precisely, and three survive only in fragments.

The *Gest* consists of 456 four-line stanzas and is divided into eight 'fyttes'. The action opens in Barnsdale and closes there and in the nearby nunnery of Kirklees. In between it ranges far and wide, from (probably) Wyredale in Lancashire to York, Nottingham and London. Little John, identifying himself to the Sheriff of Nottingham, says he was born in Holderness in the East Riding of Yorkshire. Nowhere in the *Gest* is there any mention of Sherwood. However, *Robin Hood and the Monk* specifically mentions 'mery Scherwode', while *Robin Hood and the Potter* mentions Wentbridge (in Barnsdale) at the beginning, but then focuses on Nottingham and an unnamed forest. The geographical references in the *Gest* are very specific for the Yorkshire area – the Sayles, Watling Street, Doncaster, St Mary's Abbey in York, Kirklees – but very general with regard to Nottingham and its surroundings.

Various explanations have been proposed. The two areas of Barnsdale and Sherwood are not so far apart that they could not have been traversed by one body of outlaws. But it might also be the case that exploits dealing with originally separate figures and locations came to be linked with the one name. Some of the adventures attributed to Robin Hood have been related to other historical, legendary and literary figures. Indeed, there are parallels with such heroes as Hereward the Wake, Fulke Fitzwarin, Eustace the Monk and William Wallace as well as with the ballad *Adam Bell, Clim of the Clough, and William of Cloudesly.* We cannot regard all of Robin's exploits as being unique to him. Recently Brian Lewis has suggested that 'Nottingham' is a code-name for the centre of political power that is, curiously, never mentioned in the area close to Barnsdale, namely Pontefract. The earliest historians to mention Robin Hood are fifteenth- and sixteenth-century by date and Scottish. Two of them – Andrew of Wyntoun and Walter Bower – locate him in Barnsdale, while the third, John Major, does not specify any particular locality. None of the three mentions Nottingham or Sherwood. Although these early ballads and two of the historians emphasize Barnsdale, later ballads, plays and novels have placed greater stress on Sherwood and Nottingham.

The *Gest* is fundamental to our understanding of Robin Hood. He is introduced as 'a gode yeman' and 'a prude outlaw', although no reason is given for his outlawry. Little John is the first of his 'merry men', followed by William Scarlock or Scathelock, Much the miller's son and Gilbert with the white hand. These are the only ones named; there is no Friar Tuck or Maid Marian. Robin is a deeply devout man, hearing three masses a day and being especially devoted to 'Our dere Lady'. He is concerned not to harm any woman, husbandman, yeoman, or squire, but he has it in for bishops, archbishops, monks and the High Sheriff of Nottingham. Such, then, are the premises for the events to be related.

The first main story centres on the poor unnamed knight who is in debt to St Mary's Abbey in York and tells how Robin helps him. The second story focuses on Little John and the Sheriff of Nottingham and includes the help given to the outlaws by Sir Richard at the Lee. The third story concerns the encounter of Robin with the king, in which Robin declares his loyalty and is taken into service at court. However, Robin becomes unhappy there and returns to Barnsdale, where he lives for twenty-two years before being treacherously killed at the hands of the Prioress of Kirklees and Sir Roger of Doncaster.

In the *Gest* the king is named as Edward, 'our cumly kynge', and modern historians have argued for this to be Edward II (1307-27) on the grounds that only he undertook a visit to the north of England such as is alluded to in stanza 357. 'Plomton Parke' is probably Plumpton Park near Knaresborough rather than in Cumberland, as some scholars have thought. This would be yet another Yorkshire connection.

Robin and Maid Marian *(from item 18).*

Is this then the period in which we can believe Robin Hood to have lived? Some historians have thought so. In 1852 Joseph Hunter proposed the identification of the literary Robin Hood with a Robertus Hood who appears in the court rolls of the manor of Wakefield during Edward's reign. He assumed this to be the same person as a Robyn Hod who was in service as a porter of the chamber with the king in 1323-24. He interpreted the details of the *Gest* as if it were a historical document rather than a piece of literature, and then looked in appropriate records for confirmatory names. His researches were amplified by J.W. Walker in *The True History of Robin Hood* (1952). We have to remember, however, that Robert or Robin (the diminutive of Robert) Hood was a common name in late medieval England. It is unlikely that the many occurrences of the name in historical documents will ever do more than tally with one detail of the literary Robin Hood's career. There is no evidence, for example, that the Wakefield Robertus Hood mentioned above was ever an outlaw.

Robin Hood is nowhere mentioned in any contemporary or near-contemporary English chronicles. The first references by chroniclers come from Scotland, and they are quite clearly concerned with the man we know from the ballads. Each places Robin Hood in a different period. Andrew of Wyntoun, writing between 1420 and 1424, says 1283-85; Walter Bower, writing in the 1440s, makes it 1266; while John Major (1521) places him in the reign of Richard I. It is strange that these historical accounts surface between 140 and 320 years after the dates they propose. (The same pattern, incidentally, is true with regard to William Tell. The earliest work to document him came about 150 years after the period at which he is supposed to have lived, following which the details are elaborated.) John Major's dating has proved the most popular. The great majority of retellers of the Robin Hood stories have fixed on Richard the Lionheart as his king. The crusading king, ransomed from Austrian captivity, had obvious attractions.

The quest for a historical Robin Hood does not, however, rest with considerations of the early ballads, chronicles and other scraps of literary references. Historians of the nineteenth and twentieth centuries have, in the course of other researches, turned up a good many occurrences of the name of Robert or Robin Hood in historical archives. Joseph Hunter's work has already been mentioned. A Robert Hod, fugitive, was found by L.V.D. Owen in the records of the York assizes in 1225-27. This is the only such occurrence of the name to identify Robin Hood as an outlaw. Since then eight instances of the surname or cognomen Robinhood have been discovered in documents dating between 1261-62 and 1296. Most of these are applied to criminals. Their occurrence points to the circulation of some form of story or stories about Robin Hood at an earlier date that allowed the name to be transferred to or used of a man who shared something of the famous figure's transgressions of the law. The content of such stories remains unknown.

Robin, Allen a Dale and Friar Tuck *(from item 18)*.

It is clear from the literary evidence that the stories told about Robin Hood have changed and been added to over the centuries. What is told in the *Gest* about Edward 'our cumly kynge' is an expression of fifteenth-century perceptions of the story, not an incontestable fact about the 'original' Robin Hood, who, if he is a single historical figure, looks as though he must have lived in the late twelfth and early thirteenth centuries. We can say very little about the content of his biography, his parentage, place of birth or area of his activity. The only fact that has not been contested is the traditional place of his death at Kirklees Priory. But before we look at that in more detail we must turn to his social background.

The Gentrification of Robin Hood

Although the early ballads and the chronicles portray Robin as a freeborn yeoman, the antiquary John Leland, writing in the 1530s, refers to him as a *nobilis exlex,* a noble outlaw, with no further comment. The English historian Richard Grafton, writing in 1568-69 and invoking 'an olde and auncient Pamphlet' as his source, gives more detail. He claims that Robin was 'discended of a noble parentage: or rather beyng of a base stocke and linage, was for his manhoode and chiualry aduaunced to the noble dignitie of an Erle'. Through excessive expenditure he fell into debt and was outlawed, then gathering a company of 'Roysters and Cutters' and turning to robbery in 'the forestes or wilde Countries'. Grafton is the first to discuss Robin's raised social status, but he does it ambiguously. He claims first that Robin is noble by birth, but contradicts himself immediately and says that he earned it through deeds of manhood and chivalry. However, he is unable to conduct himself appropriately and becomes an outlaw. Grafton is a historian and prepared to present varying traditions about Robin Hood, but by the end of the sixteenth century his alternative background is set to become the norm at the hands of a dramatist.

In his two plays *The Downfall of Robert Earl of Huntington* and *The Death of Robert Earl of Huntington*, written in 1598 and first published in 1601, Anthony Munday was the first to identify Robin as Earl of Huntington. This major change was followed by countless later writers. It was the decisive step in the gentrification of the popular hero. The title of Earl of Huntingdon had actually been held by David of Scotland, younger brother of King William of Scotland, in the late twelfth century, but the present title was only created in 1529. Several recent Earls have had 'Robin Hood' incorporated in their personal names.

Munday's plays present a fundamentally different picture of Robin from anything previously provided by the early ballads and plays. In making Robin a nobleman he was able to make a tragic drama, something that would have been impossible with a yeoman hero. Tragedies required noble protagonists to fulfil the rules of the genre. The earlier Robin Hood plays could have a yeoman as their hero because they were comedies. Not only did Munday make Robin into Robert Earl of Huntington, but he turned the Marian of the folk plays into Matilda, daughter of Lord Fitzwater, who is pursued by Prince (later King) John, the brother of King Richard I. Munday had taken Matilda and his basic plot from Michael Drayton's historical poem *Matilda, the Faire and Chaste Daughter of Lord R. Fitzwater* (1594). His ennoblement of both Robin and Marian changed the course of subsequent reworkings of the traditional stories. But it was not the only change made in this period.

The oldest sources are silent on the place of Robin Hood's birth and his parentage, but a manuscript life written *c.* 1600 and known as the Sloane manuscript, now in the British Library, places Robin's birth at 'Lockesley in yorkeshyre, or after others in Nottinghamsh. in ye dayes of Henry ye 2nd about ye yeare 1160'. The Sloane manuscript does not have any independent historical value, being simply a prose version of material otherwise known in ballad form. The reference to Locksley presumably comes from the ballad entitled *Robin Hood's Birth, Breeding, Valour, and Marriage*, which states:

In Locksly town, in merry Nottinghamshire,
In merry sweet Locksly town,
There bold Robin Hood he was born and bred,
Bold Robin of famous renown.

Since there is no Locksley in Nottinghamshire and only a hamlet called Loxley in Yorkshire (north-west of Sheffield), the name can hardly be regarded as factual and historical. Nonetheless, it has resulted in the name of Locksley being given to Robin in a whole slew of later forms of the stories, most notably in Sir Walter Scott's *Ivanhoe.*

We can thus discern in the sixteenth and seventeenth centuries a tendency for new 'facts' about varying aspects of Robin's life to be produced and for the episodic adventures related in the ballads to be linked as parts of a chronologically interpreted life. This process is already evident in the *Gest.* It is both a literary and a historical process. Unfortunately, the historians of the sixteenth to the eighteenth centuries relied more on imagination and intuition than on documentary evidence.

We must now return to the matter of Robin Hood's death at Kirklees. This already appears at the end of the *Gest* and is the subject of a separate ballad known in two somewhat divergent versions. Grafton mentions the fact that the Prioress of Kirklees

> caused him to be buried by the high way side, where he had vsed to rob and spoyle those that passed that way. And vpon his graue the sayde Prioresse did lay a very fayre stone, wherein the names of Robert Hood, William of Goldesborough, and others were grauen.

This gravestone is referred to by several later historians, but when Richard Gough included a drawing of it in his *Sepulchral Monuments* (1786) the inscription was no longer legible.

More troublesome than this, however, is the epitaph recorded by Thomas Gale, Dean of York 1697-1702, which reads:

Hear undernead dis laitl stean
laiz robert earl of Huntingtun
near arcir ver az hie sa geud
and pipl kauld im robin heud
sick utlawz az hi an iz men
vil england nivr si agen.

obiit 24 kal dekembris 1247

This is a fraud. The language is confused and illiterate; the date is an impossible one according to the Roman calendar; and the allusion to 'robert earl of Huntingtun' occurs nowhere in literary sources before Munday. In the nineteenth century a new gravestone with these lines was erected in the grounds of the Kirklees estate. The wording recorded by Gale is close to that given by the ballad-writer Martin Parker at the end of *A True Tale of Robin Hood* (1632):

Robert Earle of Huntington
Lies under this little stone.
No archer was like him so good:
His wildnesse named him Robbin Hood.
Full thirteene yeares, and something more,
These northerne parts he vexed sore.
Such out-lawes as he and his men
May England never know agen.

Parker, however, gives the date as 'Decembris quarto die, 1198; anno regni Richardii primi 9'. Gale's epitaph looks like a crude attempt to medievalize Parker, who is simply combining what he found in the ballads and Munday.

This preoccupation with the Kirklees gravestones and the epitaph is part and parcel of the antiquarian interest in Robin Hood, which is evident from the sixteenth century onwards and is documented in chronicles and poems such as Drayton's *Poly-Olbion* (1622). It reaches its apogee in William Stukeley's preposterous genealogy of 'Robert Fitzooth, commonly called Robin Hood, pretended Earl of Huntington, *ob.* 1274' (1274 is a misprint for 1247), published in 1746. Stukeley's work, historically aberrant though it is, has nonetheless made its mark on a number of subsequent literary forms of the story, in which the name Robert Fitzooth continues to crop up. It was aided in this by Joseph Ritson, the first scholarly editor of the Robin Hood ballads, who included it in his construction of Robin's biography.

Anyone who has studied the evolution of the literary works relating to Robin Hood and the attempts of historians to pin him down as a historical figure knows how closely intertwined these two enterprises are. The absence of biographical information in the early ballads is a spur to invention and imaginative reconstruction. Poets and storytellers, antiquaries and historians have not ceased from trying to fill this vacuum and are still at work today. However, the quest for a historical Robin Hood can only go so far. It is not the key to his continuing popularity.

Robin, the Merry Men and Maid Marian

They may be outlaws and thus cut off from ordinary society, but Robin and his companions are having a good time. They are 'merry men'. The ballads are, for the most part, celebrations of male camaraderie. The men's life in the forest is a spring-and-summertime pastoral idyll. Shakespeare describes it in *As You Like It* as 'the golden world' in which they 'fleet the time carelessly'. Robin is acknowledged as leader, but in the various ballads in which he first meets his companions he never defeats them or is able to defeat them. He recognizes their stalwart strength and invites them to join him in the greenwood.

First among Robin's companions is Little John, the only one of the merry men to be mentioned by all three Scottish chroniclers and Grafton. He appears in *Robin Hood and the*

Monk, Robin Hood and the Potter and of course the *Gest* as Robin's right-hand man. The *Gest* includes his adventures with the Sheriff of Nottingham under the name of Reynold Greenleaf. Little John is also present at Robin's death, his most trusted companion. The two are virtually inseparable. They are like David and Jonathan, Roland and Oliver. In all the early ballads Little John is with Robin from the start, so it seems. It is not until the early seventeenth century that we get a ballad, *Robin Hood and Little John*, that deals with their first meeting. Little John is described as 'seven foot high' and gives his name as John Little, which is then converted into an ironic nickname. He fights Robin with a staff on a bridge and knocks him into the water. In other places he can shoot as well as any. Tradition associates Little John with Hathersage in Derbyshire, where he is supposed to be buried.

Robin wins an archery contest in the presence of the King and 'Queen Katherine' *(from item 19).*

Among Robin's other well-known companions are Will Scarlet, Much the miller's son and Gilbert with the white hand, all of whom figure in the *Gest.* Will Stutely is mentioned in *Robin Hood and Little John* and *Robin Hood Rescuing Will Stutely*, both seventeenth-century ballads. Scarlet's name is found in various forms – Scarlok and Scathelock – out of which Anthony Munday created Scarlet and Scathlock as brothers. The figure of the Pinder of Wakefield, George a Green, the hero of an independent story, is co-opted in *The Jolly Pinder of Wakefield, with Robin Hood, Scarlet, and John*, as well as being mentioned elsewhere. None of these figures is rounded out or developed in the early ballads, although later writers have tried to differentiate them in personality. Two other figures remain – Friar Tuck and Maid Marian – about whom there is more to say.

Both Friar Tuck and Maid Marian seem to have been incorporated into the Robin Hood stories through the May games, although the name 'Friar Tuck' is used as a criminal alias as early as 1417 by a chaplain of Lindfield in Sussex. Shakespeare refers to 'the bare scalp of Robin Hood's fat friar' in *Two Gentlemen of Verona* in a scene involving outlaws (IV, i), but does not use the name 'Tuck'. The famous story of Robin's encounter with the friar was probably current in the mid-fifteenth century, but the earliest two ballad forms, usually known as *Robin Hood and the Curtal Friar*, are seventeenth-century in date. The ballads anachronistically associate the friar with Fountains Abbey, a Cistercian monastery, and with Fountains Dale. Local patriotism in Nottinghamshire has claimed Fountain Dale, near Mansfield, to be the site, but this is doubtful in view of the fact that Fountain Dale is not recorded as a place-name before 1826. There are enough inconsistencies in the ballads for doubts still to remain. The figure of Tuck gained additional resonance in Scott's *Ivanhoe* as the clerk of Copmanhurst.

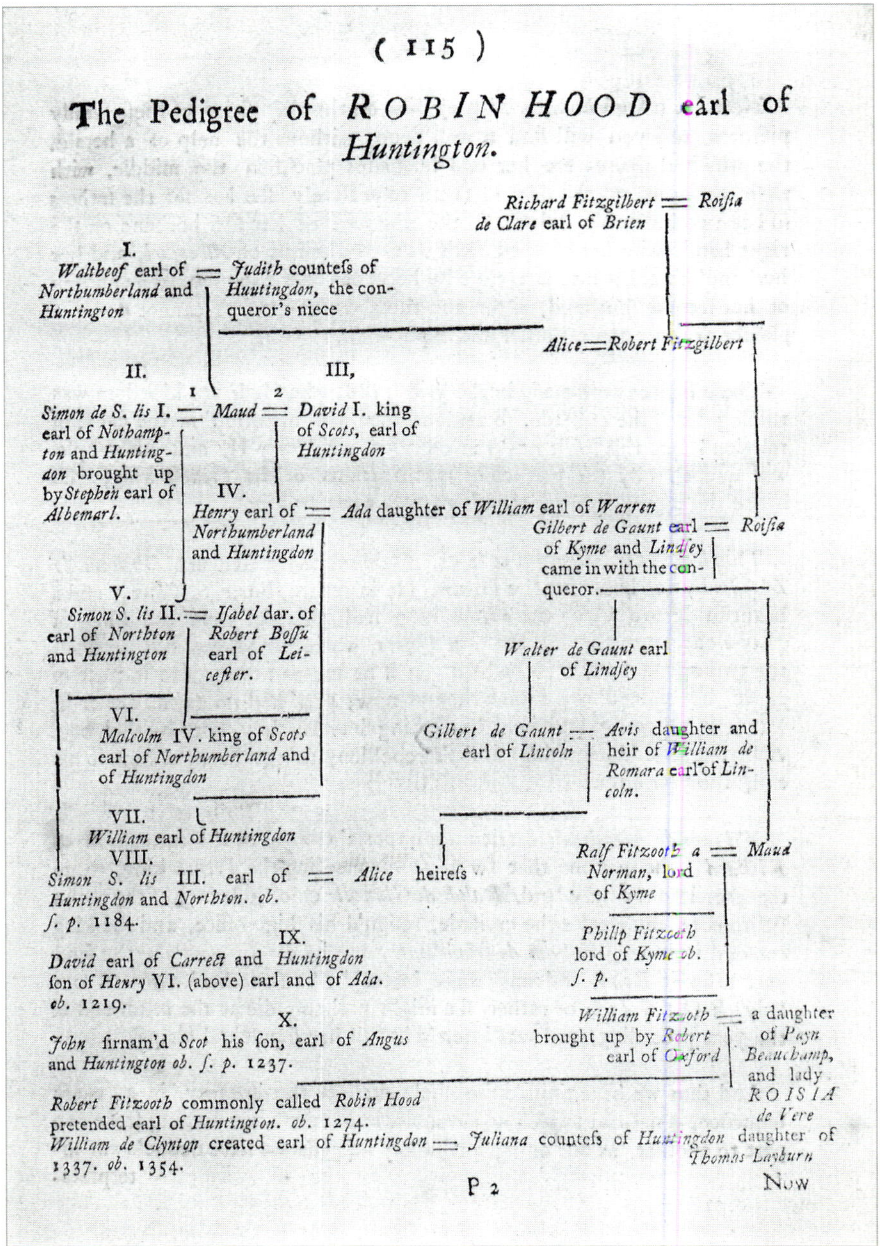

(115)

The Pedigree of *ROBIN HOOD* earl of *Huntington.*

Richard Fitzgilbert de Clare earl of *Brien* = *Roisia*

I.
Waltheof earl of *Northumberland* and *Huntington* = *Judith* countess of *Huutingdon*, the conqueror's niece

Alice = *Robert Fitzgilbert*

II.
Simon de S. lis I. earl of *Nothampton* and *Huntingdon* brought up by *Stephen* earl of *Albemarl.* = 1 *Maud* 2 = III. *David* I. king of *Scots*, earl of *Huntingdon*

IV.
Henry earl of *Northumberland* and *Huntingdon* = *Ada* daughter of *William* earl of *Warren*

Gilbert de Gaunt earl of *Kyme* and *Lindsey* came in with the conqueror. = *Roisia*

V.
Simon S. lis II. earl of *Northton* and *Huntington* = *Isabel* dar. of *Robert Bossu* earl of *Leicester.*

Walter de Gaunt earl of *Lindsey*

VI.
Malcolm IV. king of *Scots* earl of *Northumberland* and of *Huntingdon*

Gilbert de Gaunt earl of *Lincoln* = *Avis* daughter and heir of *William de Romara* earl of *Lincoln.*

VII.
William earl of *Huntingdon*

VIII.
Simon S. lis III. earl of *Huntingdon* and *Northton. ob. s. p.* 1184. = *Alice* heiress

Ralf Fitzooth a *Norman*, lord of *Kyme* = *Maud*

IX.
David earl of *Carrect* and *Huntingdon* son of *Henry* VI. (above) earl and of *Ada. ob.* 1219.

Philip Fitzooth lord of *Kyme ob. s. p.*

X.
John sirnam'd *Scot* his son, earl of *Angus* and *Huntington ob. s. p.* 1237.

William Fitzooth brought up by *Robert* earl of *Oxford* = a daughter of *Payn Beauchamp*, and lady *ROISIA de Vere*

Robert Fitzooth commonly called *Robin Hood* pretended earl of *Huntington. ob.* 1274.

William de Clynton created earl of *Huntingdon* 1337. *ob.* 1354. = *Juliana* countess of *Huntingdon* daughter of *Thomas Leyburn*

P 2 Now

An imaginative pedigree of Robin Hood *(from item 29).*

This brings us to Maid Marian. It comes as a surprise to people familiar with nineteenth- and twentieth-century forms of the Robin Hood stories to learn that Marian does not appear anywhere in the early ballads. The woman who gains Robin's heart in *Robin Hood's Birth, Breeding, Valour, and Marriage*, a seventeenth-century ballad, is a 'queen of the shepherds' called Clorinda, and the marriage takes place in Tutbury, Staffordshire. Marian appears only in one other late ballad from the seventeenth century, *Robin Hood and Maid Marian*, where the two implausibly fight in disguise, Marian being dressed as a page. This ballad is very rarely found in the collections of ballads known as garlands, so Ritson does not print it in his edition.

Marian's place in the development of the legend goes back to the May games, which assimilated the convention of the pastoral lovers, shepherd Robin and shepherdess Marion. The first literary reference to Marian occurs around 1500 in an eclogue written by Alexander Barclay in which someone wishes to hear 'some mery fit of Maide Marian or els of Robin Hood'. But there is no discernible role for Marian in the early ballads. Only when Anthony Munday plays fast and loose with the traditional material and turns Robin into Robert Earl of Huntington, the hero of a serious play, is there room for a significant female role.

Here Marian is the name given to Matilda Fitzwater when she flees to the forest. While she is Robert's beloved, she is also being courted and pursued by Prince John, just as Robert is the object of Queen Elinor's attentions. It is through the genre requirements of the drama that Marian acquires importance in the Robin Hood legend. The ballads – apart from the *Gest* – are unsophisticated in plot and character portrayal, while the drama, if it is to succeed, needs greater tension and a filling-out of character. Marian is essential to the gentrification of the Robin Hood stories. She is part, too, of Ben Jonson's unfinished masque *The Sad Shepherd* but she does not really come into her own until the nineteenth century with the development of the popular novel. The original tales of Robin Hood are male adventures, trials of strength. When Marian becomes a significant figure, they are transformed into romances or love-stories. The adventures are still there, but they now serve a romantic purpose

We have taken a look at the chief figures on Robin's side. Now we must turn to the opposition. At the head is the Sheriff of Nottingham, followed by representatives of the Church – the Abbot of St Mary's, York, the Bishop of Hereford, various monks and the Prioress of Kirklees. All of them embody power; they belong to the ruling class and exercise secular and religious power, usually harshly. None of them is given a name; it is the office they hold that is the focus of the stories' attention. Between Robin and these nameless men (and a woman) we find three or four members of the knightly class – Sir Guy of Gisborne and Sir Roger of Doncaster, both opponents, and Sir Richard at the Lee and the poor knight from the beginning of the *Gest,* who has often been identified with Sir Richard anyway, both helped by Robin. The opposition is thus not determined simply by class: they are greedy, selfish exploiters of power, not honest and fair wielders of legitimate authority. This is made clear when Robin meets the disguised king in the forest and, recognizing him, immediately expresses his loyalty. It matters not whether it is Edward, as in the *Gest,* or Richard, as in most other retellings of this episode. Robin is not a man who wants to turn the world upside down and abolish the class system: he is not part of the Peasants' Revolt. What he stands for is something different.

The *Gest* stresses Robin's piety, his daily hearing of three masses, his devotion to Our Lady. As is often the case in popular literature of the Middle Ages, the hero's understanding of Christianity is direct, simple and sincere, contrasting with the exploitative conduct and worldly comfort of the high clergy. Robin tells his men not to harm the husbandman, the good yeoman or the knight and squire who can be identified as a 'gode felawe'. John Major mentions Robin's protectiveness towards women, but this plays little part in the early ballads. It may be a sign of the incipient gentrification of the stories, which is in full swing by the end of the sixteenth century. Above all, Robin stands for honesty and decency in social behaviour. He helps the knight who confesses his poverty, but he has no compunction in despoiling the monks who try to make him believe they have little money. The skill of Robin and his men with the bow and arrow is well known. It reaches its zenith in *Robin Hood and Queen Katherine*, where, under the name of Clifton, he splits a willow wand with his arrow. This is a feat performed also by William of Cloudesly in *Adam Bell, Clim of the Clough, and William of Cloudesly*, but Cloudesly, like William Tell, also can shoot an apple placed on his small son's head. Scott uses the incident to striking effect in chapter 13 of *Ivanhoe*.

With his skill in shooting and his ability to summon scores of men at the sound of his bugle, Robin is unconquerable. When he dies, it can only be through treachery or mishap, as it was with Achilles, with Roland, Siegfried, and with Jesus of Nazareth. The true hero cannot die in an ordinary way. With Robin the treachery is poignant, as it comes at the hand of 'a wycked woman' who is described as a relative. The fact that she is a prioress and the illicit beloved of Sir Roger of Doncaster (elsewhere called Red Roger) constitutes a double blow against the Church, but for Kirklees the deed has ensured lasting fame and a tangible, if spurious, monument.

Robin's exploits continued to be celebrated and expanded in ballads that were composed long after the fifteenth and early sixteenth centuries. They do not always agree with what we know from the early texts. One ballad fancifully has Robin fight the Prince of Aragon and two giants, which removes him from his normal realistic sphere of activity. Ben Jonson introduces the figure of Maudlin, the witch of Papplewick, a village on the edge of Sherwood, into *The Sad Shepherd*, and this innovation has given rise to other similar figures down the centuries right up to Richard Carpenter's television films and books, and the film, *Robin Hood, Prince of Thieves*.

While most modern forms of the stories remain resolutely realistic and historical in their portrayal of Robin, some voices have drawn attention to supposedly mythological or supernatural aspects. The name 'Hood' has been variously interpreted as to do with the hood worn by goblins or as being a corruption of 'Wood', making Robin into a spirit of the woods or perhaps an incarnation of the Green Man, who appears in medieval carvings with a head sprouting with leaves. The names of Puck and Robin Goodfellow have also been adduced, but the story of *Robin Goodfellow*, extant only from 1628, presents a kind of fairy trickster that has nothing in common with the hero of the early ballads.

Nineteenth-century folklore scholars were apt to interpret the protagonists of myths, hero-tales and fairytales in terms of nature symbolism or primitive cosmology, and Robin Hood did not escape this fashion. In the *Dictionary of National Biography* Sidney Lee totally discounts any genuine historicity with regard to Robin Hood and roundly declares that the name 'originally belonged to a mythical forest-elf'. Modern proponents of this mythological approach, such as John Matthews and Steve Wilson, are uninterested in the historical and literary aspects of Robin Hood, but co-opt him into their own 'Celtic' or 'New Age' nature spirituality. They illustrate perfectly how the Robin Hood stories contain multiple possibilities for interpretation. It is ironic that a hero who is marked in the early ballads and by the historian John Major as deeply Christian and devoted to the Virgin Mary should in the last two decades have been so comprehensively paganized. Other writers have also secularized him.

The original core of stories exemplifies a set of binary oppositions which have proved extraordinarily attractive through the centuries. They can be tabulated as follows:

forest	town
Barnsdale, Sherwood	Nottingham
yeoman and peasant	sheriff and nobility
innocent victim	wicked oppressor
devotion to Virgin Mary	treachery of prioress
laymen and friar	abbot, bishop, monks
named individuals	unnamed high office-holders
(exception: the poor knight)	(exceptions: Sir Guy of Gisborne, Sir Roger of Doncaster)
loyalty to the king	opposition to Prince John

To these may be added a further opposition which does not seem to have been articulated before *Ivanhoe*, but which appears in several forms of the story afterwards:

Saxon	Norman

The features associated with Robin cover a wide range of characteristics. In the late Middle Ages they ensured him immense popularity among the ordinary people, a popularity that has lasted to the present day, although the emphases in some of the binary oppositions have changed.

Changes in Form, Style and Audience

In the transmission of the Robin Hood stories the role of the ballads is pre-eminent. The sixteenth and seventeenth centuries added to the corpus, varying the stock situations and updating the material. As individual ballads were reprinted they were linguistically modernized. Collections known as 'garlands' were made, the earliest dating from 1663 (London: W. Gilbertson). Their content was not fixed. When Joseph Ritson made his first scholarly edition of ballad texts in 1795, it contained thirty-three items. Ritson's collection went through many editions in the nineteenth century. Other scholarly editions were made by J.M. Gutch in 1847 and Francis James Child in 1888 (as part of his five-volume edition of *The English and Scottish Popular Ballads*). Individual ballads have continued to be printed and illustrated in anthologies designed for the general reader and for children right up to the present day. The ballads are thus the most durable of the varied literary forms in which the stories have been disseminated. Many of the prose retellings too are based principally on them, e.g. those by Carola Oman (1939) and Roger Lancelyn Green (1956).

Robin, disguised as a palmer, visits Will Scarlet in the condemned cell *(from item 39)*.

Robin's men give their allegiance to Richard I, who has come disguised as a priest *(from item 45).*

number and attractiveness. The period also saw a growth in the chapbook industry. Numerous authors, including Wordsworth, Coleridge, Crabbe and Clare, testify to their childhood reading of chapbook tales of popular heroes, among them Robin Hood. By the early 1800s, if not before, tales of Robin Hood, usually severely abbreviated, were being published specifically for children. Sometimes the illustrations would be hand-coloured, a job done by children round a table for a pittance. Such chapbooks continued to be published

Friar Tuck throws Robin in the river *(from item 71).*

up to about 1850. They mark the beginnings of what has been, throughout the twentieth century, the most extensively cultivated target audience for our medieval hero.

Enthusiasts for appealingly-presented books for the young in the 1840s were the go-ahead publisher Joseph Cundall and the antiquarian-scholar W.J. Thoms, the latter of whom did his work under the pseudonym of Ambrose Merton. In 1840 Cundall, using the pseudonym Stephen Percy, published his own *Robin Hood and his Merry Foresters*, which was lithographically illustrated by John Gilbert. He also published Thoms's (Merton's) *The Old Story Books of England* (1845), which included both *A True Tale of Robin Hood* (adapted from Martin Parker) and *The Mad Pranks of Robin Goodfellow*. The illustrations in this latter book appeared in both black-and-white and coloured editions. Illustrations were now a key element in the presentation of the tales. In *Robin Hood and his Merry Men* (London: Frederick Warne & Co., *c.* 1867), one in a series entitled 'Aunt Louisa's London Toy Books', the colour-printed illustrations are the most important part of the book; the stories are reduced to a bare minimum. Once cheap colour-printing could be used in children's books, publishers relied on illustrations to sell them. New pictures could sell an old story.

Despite this emphasis on colour illustration aimed at the younger end of the market, many children's novels were written for older readers. John B. Marsh's *The Life and Adventures of Robin Hood* went through at least eight editions from *c.* 1865 until after the First World War. Also popular were stories by William Heaton and Henry Gilbert, the latter's text being produced in different editions, from 1912 with illustrations by Walter Crane to the 1950s without illustration. Versions by E. Charles Vivian (illustrated by Harry G. Theaker) and J. Walker McSpadden and Charles Wilson (more subtly illustrated by N.C. Wyeth) dominated the early part of the twentieth century for teenage readers. Younger ones had a 'Books for the Bairns' retelling, with line-drawings by Brinsley Le Fanu (1906), along with versions by H.E. Marshall, F.C. Tilney and Rose Yeatman Woolf to entertain them.

Although Robin Hood is a characteristically English folk hero, his fame has certainly spread outside Britain. Alexandre Dumas has already been mentioned, and German scholars and men of letters were writing about Robin Hood in the nineteenth century, even translating some of the ballads. A major contribution was made by American writers and artists, beginning with Howard Pyle in 1883. His version, with his own strong line-drawings, has been reprinted for more than a century and is thus one of the most long-lived. Two other American books appeared in the first decade of the twentieth century, by Eva March Tappan (1903) and Elinor M. Buckingham (1910). The version by McSpadden, Wilson and Wyeth was also an American production from the same period (1904), and it enjoyed great popularity in Britain too, as already noted.

Most of the authors up to the 1930s are not famous as writers of other books for children. But it is a curious fact that from this time on we have several Robin Hood books by writers who have since been recognized as the leading authors of the period. Enid Blyton, the most popular children's author of the century, wrote various Robin Hood books, including plays, between 1927 and 1935, reprints following up to the 1960s. They are not, however, among her best-known work. In *Bows Against the Barons* (1934) Geoffrey Trease wrote one of the most original contributions to the theme. It was one of his earliest books and avoided a direct retelling of the traditional stories, preferring instead to create a new story connected with Robin but focused on a peasant boy called Dickon. It was also innovative in taking a strong Marxist approach to the material, interpreting Robin's actions as fighting for the peasantry against the exploitative upper classes and the Church. Carola Oman's *Robin Hood, the Prince of Outlaws* came out in 1937. Rosemary Sutcliff's *The Chronicles of Robin Hood* (1950) was actually her first published book. Perhaps the most widely diffused version from the mid-century is Roger Lancelyn Green's *The Adventures of Robin Hood*, first published in Puffin Books in 1956 and still in print.

Making Robin Hood known to the younger reader has involved all kinds of adaptations and techniques. Magazine format with the additional invention of new adventures goes back to the late nineteenth century. The 'Classics illustrated' *Robin Hood* from Strato Publications of Oadby is just one example of the genre from the 1950s. This period following the Second World War also saw a series of *Robin Hood Annuals* with strip-cartoon stories, many newly invented, and background information about medieval history and comparable heroes. There have been books for every level of reading ability, ranging from a simplified single story to longer narratives of the traditional material and new stories that presume an acquaintance with the tradition but credit Robin with fresh exploits.

Authors have become increasingly aware of the need to capture the young reader's imagination, realizing that simply retelling the old stories is, usually, not enough. This has led to a more prominent role for Marian, a feature that is not just a reflection of feminist concerns in the 1980s and '90s, but goes back much earlier. Michael Morpurgo's *Robin of Sherwood* (1960) makes use of the time-travel theme so that the stories form part of a boy's vivid dream experience. Tilman Röhrig's German retelling, *Robin Hood: solang es Unrecht gibt* (1994), is another fine example of a creative approach to the material. It is surprising that it has not been translated into English. Many of the more recent books are magnificently illustrated. Among the artists Victor Ambrus, Patrick Benson and Michael Foreman really stand out.

Most children's books present Robin Hood seriously, telling a historically-based, credible story. The style and narrative technique will vary according to the target readership and the skill of the author. This is true too of the many Robin Hood films that have been made since 1908. Films, television, popular plays and pantomimes play only a small part in this exhibition, because the focus is chiefly on printed material, but they are hugely important in the dissemination of the Robin Hood legend. Films in particular are able to project powerful images and ideals, but they have also, especially towards the end of this century, incorporated a kind of jokiness and burlesque that surfaces in dramatic forms of the stories from the late medieval plays onwards. While Robin is taken seriously as a folk hero, the stories are so well known that they can easily be guyed and satirized. Two recent children's books exemplify this humorous approach. One is Nick Bantock's little pop-up rhyme book, the other Marcia Williams's strip-cartoon version of 1995. Both books only function fully if the reader is already acquainted with Robin Hood. Appreciation depends on some degree of understanding of what has been done to tradition. With the serious books the stories can be read independently, but Bantock and Williams are intertextual in their construction.

Robin Hood has never been more alive than he is today. Not only does he flourish in books and films, on television and the stage, but visitor centres such as Tales of Robin Hood in Nottingham use him to expound medieval social and political history. Robin is a very marketable product. Even a local railway has been named the Robin Hood Line. In addition, he has been the subject of numerous books and articles by historians and literary scholars, folklorists and enthusiasts. If he still escapes being pinned down and trapped by them, it is not for want of effort or skill. Since Robin Hood was first mentioned by Langland there has been a never-ending stream of ballads and stories, plays and other performances in which he has delighted the public. Every age has created a picture of Robin for itself documenting social and political changes, and different attitudes towards class and gender, masculinity, power and officialdom. While every reworking keeps faith with a medieval Robin Hood and does not transplant him to some other time or place, the stock cast of characters and their confrontations allow for both identification and differentiation on the part of author and audience. There is an openness or looseness in the texture of the material that invites creative participation. That is why Robin Hood can be a hero for all times.

Further Reading

The secondary literature on Robin Hood is enormous. The books listed here are a small selection that I have found particularly useful in preparing this exhibition. Each contains further substantial bibliographical material.

Kevin Carpenter (ed.), *Robin Hood. Die vielen Gesichter des edlen Räubers. The Many Faces of that Celebrated English Outlaw* (Oldenburg: Bibliotheks- und Informationssystem der Universität Oldenburg, 1995). This is the catalogue of the massive exhibition organized by Kevin Carpenter at the University of Oldenburg, Germany, including many illustrations and fourteen essays by various writers. The book is bilingual; English translations or summaries are given of all the German material. The exhibition travelled to Poland, Switzerland, Denmark, the Netherlands and Berlin, but it proved impossible to bring it to Britain.

R.B. Dobson and J. Taylor, *Rymes of Robyn Hood. An Introduction to the English Outlaw* (London: Heinemann, 1976). This provides texts or extracts of some twenty-five poems or plays, together with related material and a lengthy introduction.

J.C. Holt, *Robin Hood* (London: Thames and Hudson, revised and enlarged edition, 1989). Chiefly concerned with the debates about the historicity of Robin Hood.

Stephen Knight, *Robin Hood. A Complete Study of the English Outlaw* (Oxford, UK and Cambridge, USA: Blackwell, 1994). A detailed, mainly literary survey from the Middle Ages to the present day.

Acknowledgements

This exhibition owes its origin to two particular stimuli from the German-speaking world. Professor Werner Wunderlich of the University of St Gallen, Switzerland, invited me to write about Robin Hood for a collection of essays on medieval rulers, heroes and saints, which was published with the title *Herrscher Helden Heilige* (St Gallen: UVK, 1996). Around the same time Dr Kevin Carpenter was working on his magnificent, huge Robin Hood exhibition at the University of Oldenburg, Germany. The catalogue for that exhibition, which includes several substantial essays on diverse aspects of the Robin Hood phenomenon, has been a constant source of reference and inspiration to me. The exhibition was to have come to England, but it proved impossible to find a suitable venue and finance. This led me to consider mounting a smaller exhibition based on the holdings of the John Rylands University Library of Manchester, together with loans from private collections. The Rylands possesses many rare books that document early interest in the history of Robin Hood, while the private collections show a cross-section of a variety of publications from the past 200 years. I should like to thank Mr Brian Alderman, Mrs Pat Garret, Mr A.C. Grand and Professor Wilfried Keutsch in particular for their support and encouragement and for their gifts and loans of books. The staff of the John Rylands University Library of Manchester have, as always, been uniformly helpful and enthusiastic in working to stage this exhibition.

David Blamires

1. Early Literary Traces

1 WILLIAM LANGLAND
The Vision of Pierce Plowman
London: Roberte Crowley, 1550.
13746 *

Langland's *Piers Plowman*, written *c.* 1377, provides our earliest reference to Robin Hood as a well-known literary hero. Langland's allegorical figure Sloth declares:

> If I should dye by thys daye me lyst not to loke
> I can not parfitly mi pater noster as the preist it singeth
> But I can ryms of Robenhode & Randof erl of chester
> But of our lorde or our lady, I lerne nothing at all.
> (fol. xxvi verso)

> [If I were to die today, I should be scared to look.
> I don't know the Lord's Prayer properly as the priest chants it,
> but I do know rhymes of Robin Hood and Randolf Earl of Chester.
> But of our Lord or our Lady I'm in complete ignorance.]

However, it is not until the middle of the fifteenth century that we find the earliest surviving manuscript ballad, i.e. *Robin Hood and the Monk* (Cambridge University Library, MS Ff 5.48).

Of the other popular hero, Randolf Earl of Chester, i.e. Rannulf de Blundeville, d. 1232, no literary tales have survived, although the rough plot of two possible tales can be reconstructed from later sources.

Piers Plowman is known in a large number of fourteenth- and fifteenth-century manuscripts, but this is the first printed edition. This copy is printed on vellum.

*** Here and elsewhere the Catalogue gives the John Rylands University Library of Manchester reference number.**

2 *Dives and Pauper*
London: Richarde Pynson, 1493.
9852

This homiletic text, written between 1405 and 1410, which got into print in 1493, admonishes the frivolous:

> They haue leuer go to the tauerne than to holy church Leuyr to here a
> songe of Robynhode, or of some rybaudry. thanne to here messe or
> matyns or any other of goddes seruyce. or any Word of god
> (The firste Precepte, end of chapter li)

[They would rather go to the tavern than to church, rather hear a song of Robin Hood or of some ribaldry than hear mass or matins or any other divine service or any word of God.]

3 [SEBASTIAN BRANT]
The Shyp of Folys of the Worlde
Translated out of Laten, Frenche and Doche by Alexander Barclay.
London: Rycharde Pynson, 1509.
15412

Alexander Barclay (*c.* 1476-1552), born 'beyonde the cold river of Twede', makes three references to Robin Hood in his verse translation of Brant. In the chapter 'Of the claterynge and bablynge of prestis and clerkes in the quere' he deplores the clergy's lack of devotion:

And in the mornynge when they come to the quere
The one begynneth a Fable or a hystory
The other lenyth theyr erys it to here
Takynge it in stede of the Inuytory *
Some other maketh respons antym and memory
And all of fables and Jestis of Robyn hode
Or other tryfyls that skantly are so gode
(CLXXXXIII verso)

* *Inuytory: invitatory (psalm) or introit*

In one of his Eclogues written in 1513-14, Barclay makes the first literary allusion to Maid Marian: 'Yet would I gladly heare some mery if / Of mayde Marion, or els of Robin hood.'

4 WILLIAM SHAKESPEARE
As You Like It
In: William Shakespeare, *Comedies, Histories, & Tragedies*. Published according to the True Originall Copies.
London: printed by Isaac Iaggard and Ed. Blount, 1623.
8123

A brief reference in the opening scene of *As You Like It* (1599-1600) relates the exile of the old duke to that of Robin Hood, providing it with a nostalgic colour:

Oli[ver]: Where will the old Duke liue?

Cha[rles]: They say hee is already in the Forrest of *Arden*, many merry men with him; and there they liue like the old *Robin Hood* of *England:* they say many yong Gentlemen flocke to him euery day, and fleet the time carelessly as they did in the golden world.

5 MICHAEL DRAYTON
Poly-Olbion Great Britaine
2 vols.
London: M. Lownes, I. Browne, I. Helme, I. Burbie, [1622].
3924

In song 26 of his poetic celebration of the topography of Britain and its historical and legendary associations, Drayton has two passages, focusing on Sherwood and Wakefield, that deal with Robin Hood and his companions. No mention is made of Robin as Earl of Huntington, but Marian occupies a prominent place in his affections:

> He from the husbands bed no married woman wan,
> But to his Mistris deare, his loued *Marian*
> Was euer constant knowne, which wheresoere shee came,
> Was soueraigne of the Woods, chiefe Lady of the Game:
> Her Clothes tuck'd to the knee, and daintie braided haire,
> With Bow and Quiuer arm'd, shee wandered here and there,
> Amongst the Forrests wild; *Diana* neuer knew
> Such pleasures, nor such *Harts* as *Mariana* slew.

2. Early Texts

6 GEOFFREY CHAUCER
The Canterbury Tales
London: R. Pynson, 1490.
10002

The Prologue to *The Canterbury Tales* in Pynson's edition has a woodcut of a yeoman that was later used as a portrait of Robin Hood in the so-called Lettersnijder edition, attributed to Jan van Doesborch (National Library of Scotland, Edinburgh), printed *c.* 1510-15. Chaucer's description of the yeoman gives a good idea of how Robin Hood was first envisaged:

> a yeman hadde he and seruauntes nomo
> At that time for he list to ryde soo
> And he was cladde in cote and hode of grene
> A sheef of pecok arowes bright and shene
> Vndre his belt he bare ful thriftely
> Wele coude he dresse his takyl yomanly
> His arowes drouped nat with fethers lowe
> And in his hond he bare a mighty bowe
> A not hede he hadde with a broune bisage [visage]
> Of wodemannes craft coude he alle the bsage [vsage]

Vpon his arme he bare a gay bracer
And by his syde a suerde and a bokeler
And on that other side a gay dagger
Harnesed wele and sharp as poynte of spere
A cristofer on his brest of siluer shene
An horne he baar the bawdryk was of grene
A foster was he sothly as I gesse.
(a iiii recto and verso)

7 *A Mery Geste of Robyn Hoode and of his Lyfe, with a Newe Playe for to be Played in Maye Games Very Pleasaunte and Full of Pastyme*
London: William Copland, *c.* 1561-69.
In: *Robin Hood c. 1561-9. London: William Copland.* The Tudor Facsimile Texts, edited by John S. Farmer.
London: Tudor Facsimile Texts, 1914.
R16051

This is the most complex of the early poems about Robin Hood, being 456 stanzas long and divided into eight 'fyttes'. It goes under the name of *Gest*, *Lytell Geste* and *Mery Geste of Robyn Hoode* according to the different printers. William Copland's edition (British Library) is the latest of the sixteenth-century editions. The edition by Wynkyn de Worde (between 1492 and 1534) survives complete (Cambridge University Library), while an edition attributed to Jan van Doesborch of Antwerp (*c.* 1510-15) preserves only about half the text (National Library of Scotland, Edinburgh). Some fragments of other editions also survive.

8 *Robin Hood and the Sheriff of Nottingham*
c. 1475.
In: *The Malone Society Collections*, vol. 1.
Oxford: The Malone Society, 1911.
R13851

This dramatic fragment is contained in a manuscript in the Library of Trinity College, Cambridge. It seems to present two scenes, the first of which reflects the action of the ballad of *Robin Hood and Guy of Gisborne*, known to us from the later manuscript that Thomas Percy first published in his *Reliques*. The second scene provides us with the earliest mention in literature of Friar Tuck.

9 ANTHONY MUNDAY
The Downfall of Robert Earl of Huntington
With illustrations and notes by J. Payne Collier.
London: Septimus Prowett, 1828.
In: *Five Old Plays*, forming a supplement to the collections of Dodsley and others. Edited by J. Payne Collier.
London: William Pickering, 1833.
23123

This play and its companion piece *The Death of Robert Earl of Huntington* by Anthony Munday were first published in 1601. Munday was the first person to identify Robin Hood as Earl of Huntington. The action of the two plays takes place during King Richard I's absence in the Holy Land and is largely occupied with Robin's relationship with Matilda, daughter of Lord Fitzwater, who is also being pursued by Richard's brother, Prince John. Matilda is frequently called Marian, and her role in these plays has proved enduringly influential in later developments of the figure of Marian.

3. The Ballad Tradition to the Mid-Nineteenth Century

10 [MARTIN PARKER]
A True Tale of Robin Hood
In: *The Old Story Books of England*, collected and re-edited by Ambrose Merton. Illustrated with twelve pictures by eminent artists.
London: Chapman and Hall, *c.* 1850.
Private collection

A True Tale of Robin Hood was the work of the professional ballad-writer Martin Parker (*c.* 1600 - *c.* 1656) and first published in London by T. Coles in 1632. It portrays Robin as the outlawed Earl of Huntington in the period of Richard I (following Grafton) and synthesizes material from several sources. The clergy are particularly vilified, the Abbot of St Mary's and the Bishop of Ely, Richard's viceroy, being singled out. Robin is bled to death by a faithless friar, not the Prioress of Kirklees. Robin's help to the poor and those in distress is specially emphasized.

Ambrose Merton, the pseudonym of W.J. Thoms, reduces Parker's 120 stanzas to ninety-three, removing much of the animus against the clergy as well as repetition. The illustration is by Frederick Taylor (1802-89).

11 *Robin Hood and the Bishop*
In: *The Roxburghe Ballads,* with short notes by Wm. Chappell. Vol. 2.
Hertford: The Ballad Society, 1874.
R17394

Robin Hood and the Bishop was published in London by W.O. some time during the reign of Charles II. Its subtitle gives the content: 'Shewing how Robin Hood went to an Old Woman's House and changed Cloaths with her, to escape from the Bishop; and how he robbed him of all his Gold, and made him sing Mass.' It was usual for ballads to be printed and sold separately during the seventeenth and eighteenth centuries, and the Roxburghe collection contains four other such Robin Hood ballads.

12 *Reliques of Ancient English Poetry. Consisting of Old Heroic Ballads, Songs, and Other Pieces of our Earlier Poets, Together with Some Few of Later Date*
[Edited by Thomas Percy.]
Fourth edition.
3 vols.
London: F. and C. Rivington, 1794.
11594

The first edition of Percy's *Reliques* (1765) provided the first printing of *Robin Hood and Guy of Gisborne*, taken from a manuscript now in the British Library. The ballad belongs to the earliest stock of Robin Hood poems and is probably late medieval in date.

13 *Old Ballads, Historical and Narrative, with Some of Modern Date*
Now first collected, and reprinted from rare copies and MSS. with notes by Thomas Evans.
Second edition.
4 vols.
London: T. Evans, 1784.
R97329

In the wake of Percy's *Reliques*, Thomas Evans printed twenty-seven Robin Hood ballads in volume 1 of this large collection, which was first published in 1777.

14 *Robin Hood's Garland. Being a Complete History of All the Notable and Merry Exploits Performed by him and his Men on Many Occasions...*
Adorned with twenty-seven neat and curious cuts adapted to the subject of each song.
London: J. Marshall and Co., *c.* 1790.
Private collection

This *Garland*, like most others, opens with *The Pedigree, Education, and Marriage of Robin Hood with Clorinda, Queen of Titbury Feast* and makes no mention of Maid Marian. Although the preface locates Robin's activities during the time that King Richard I was away on the crusade, it gives his death as 'about the latter end of 1395', probably a misprint for 1195. The place is given variously as 'Birkleys' and 'Birkslay', a misapprehension that may go back to Richard Grafton, who has 'Bircklies'. Each of the twenty-seven ballads is decorated with a small wood engraving, one used three times.

15 *Robin Hood: a Collection of All the Ancient Poems, Songs, and Ballads, now Extant, Relative to that Celebrated Outlaw: to which are Prefixed Historical Anecdotes of his Life*
[By Joseph Ritson.]
2 vols.
London: T. Egerton and J. Johnson, 1795.
9160

Joseph Ritson (1753-1803), a noted antiquary and scholar, was the first person to produce a critical edition of the Robin Hood ballads with all the apparatus of scholarship. It was reprinted and adapted in many editions throughout the nineteenth century. In addition to the texts of thirty-three ballads Ritson sketched a biography that has proved fruitful for the fictional development of Robin Hood, although it is historically highly questionable.

Each of the ballads is illustrated with a wood engraving by Thomas Bewick (1753-1828) at the beginning and end of the piece. The wood engravings exhibited illustrate *A Lytell Geste of Robin Hood* and *Robin Hood's Death and Burial.*

16 *Robin Hood's Garland. Being a Complete History of All the Notable and Merry Exploits Performed by him and his Men, on Divers Occasions...*
Stirling: C. Randall, 1811.
R101554.1/3

This chapbook collection of twenty-six ballads opens with *The Pedigree, Education, and Marriage of Robin with Clarinda Queen of Titbury Feast* and makes no mention of Maid Marian. Despite the book's inclusion of two late ballads, the preface places Robin in Richard I's time and dates his death 'about the latter end of 1195'.

17 *Historical Anecdotes of the Life of Robin Hood; with a Collection of the Ancient Poems, Songs and Ballads Relative to that Celebrated English Outlaw*
London: printed for the Booksellers. William Walker, Otley, 1846.
R146096

A substantial life of Robin Hood is followed by the texts of nineteen ballads, beginning with the *Lytell Geste* and including *Robin Hood and Maid Marian.*

4. Ballads in the Nineteenth and Twentieth Centuries

18 *The Life and Exploits of Robin Hood: and Robin Hood's Garland*
Halifax: Milner and Sowerby, 1859.
Private collection

In addition to modernized texts of thirty-four ballads, including the oldest, this anonymously edited book provides a prose version derived from them. The editor also summarizes Ritson's biography of Robin Hood, only to reject it completely and locate him as living in the reigns of Henry III and Edward I. The book is rounded off with ten further Robin Hood poems written or first published in the eighteenth and nineteenth centuries. The Halifax firm of Milner and Sowerby was one of the leading publishers of cheap popular books for the masses.

19 *Old English Ballads. A Collection of Favourite Ballads of the Olden Time*
With fifty illustrations by Birket Foster, Joseph Nash, Frederick Tayler, George Thomas, John Absolon, and John Franklin.
London: Ward, Lock, and Tyler, *c.* 1870.
Private collection

This collection includes five Robin Hood ballads among its total of forty-seven. *Robin Hood and Queen Katherine,* a late ballad known from the collection of Anthony à Wood (1632-95), focuses on a shooting match in Finsbury Field and features the Queen's page, Richard Patrington, Sir Richard Lee, the Bishop of Herefordshire, Midge the miller's son, and Little John as well as Robin and the Queen.

Robin returns from the hunt *(from item 10)*.

Robin kills Guy of Gisborne *(from item 20).*

The wedding of Allen a Dale *(from item 21).*

Robin and Will Gamewell overpower two foresters as Maid Marian looks on *(from item 49).*

Robin fights with Little John *(from item 50).*

Robin's archers to the rescue! *(from item 75)*.

The outlaws bring a captive to Robin *(from item 78)*.

Robin features in a twentieth-century children's book *(from item 83).*

20 *The Book of Brave Old Ballads*
Illustrated with sixteen coloured engravings, from drawings by John Gilbert.
London: Ward, Lock, and Tyler, [1870].
Private collection

Three out of fifteen ballads in this selection deal with Guy of Gisborne, the Curtal Friar and Allen a Dale. John Gilbert (1817-97), a prolific artist and illustrator, was knighted in 1872.

21 *Robin Hood. His Deeds and Adventures as Recounted in the Old English Ballads*
Selected and illustrated by Lucy Fitch Perkins.
London and Edinburgh: T.C. and E.C. Jack, [1906].
Private collection

Lucy Fitch Perkins (1865-1937), an American illustrator, provides twelve rather nostalgic designs in subtle colours for ten of the best-known ballads.

Robin Hood and Allen a Dale survives in broadsides of the late seventeenth century, but the episode described is referred to in the prose life of Robin Hood known as the Sloane manuscript (*c.* 1600). There, however, the young lover is named as Scarlock. The figure of Allen a Dale is thus a late addition to Robin's entourage.

22 *A Bundle of Ballads*
Compiled by Ruth Manning-Sanders.
Illustrated by William Stobbs.
London: Oxford University Press, 1959.
Private collection

Nine Robin Hood ballads are included in this generous selection designed for children. William Stobbs (b. 1914) has produced striking illustrations for many children's books. *Robin Hood and the Two Priests* goes more often under the title *Robin Hood's Golden Prize.*

23 *The Ballads of Robin Hood*
Illustrated by David Gentleman.
Edited and introduced by Jim Lees.
Cambridge: printed for members of the Limited Editions Club at the University Press, 1977.
Private collection

This book prints twenty-seven of the episodic ballads, followed by the three ballad biographies. David Gentleman (b. 1930) provides a multitude of small drawings in black and white and eight decorative lithographs. The book is open at Little John's escape from gaol in *Robin Hood and the Monk*, the earliest known of the ballads, contained in a manuscript of *c.* 1450 in Cambridge University Library.

5. What the Historians Say

24 ANDREW OF WYNTOUN

The Orygynale Cronykil of Scotland
Now first published, with notes, a glossary, &c. by David MacPherson.
London: Thomas Egerton; Edinburgh: William Laing, 1795.
8932

The *Orygynale Cronykil* of Andrew of Wyntoun (*c.* 1350 - *c.* 1424), finished between 1420 and 1424, is the first historical work to mention Robin Hood. The text is written in rhyming couplets, and the reference to Robin Hood comes in the period 1283-85:

> Lytil Jhon and Robyne Hude
> Wayth-men ware commanded gud:
> In Yngil-wode and Barnysdale
> Thai oysyd all this tyme thare trawale.

[Little John and Robin Hood were celebrated as forest outlaws. They pursued their activities all this time in Inglewood and Barnsdale.]

The Scottish chronicler is the only writer to connect Robin Hood with the Cumbrian forest of Inglewood, better known as the haunt of the other medieval outlaws Adam Bell, Clim of the Clough and William of Cloudesly.

25 JOHN FORDUN

Scotichronicon Genuinum, una cum ejusdem Supplemento ac Continuatione
Edited by Thomas Hearne.
5 vols.
Oxford: Sheldonian Theatre, 1722.
4880

In the 1440s Fordun's *Scotichronicon* was added to and continued by Walter Bower, who includes under the year 1266 a short passage on Robin Hood, locating his activities in the period of Simon de Montfort's opposition to Henry III (vol. 3 of Hearne's edition, pp. 773-4). This passage is remarkable in that it provides a summary of a story of Robin that is recorded nowhere else. This reads in English translation:

At this time there arose from the dispossessed and raised his head that most famous murderer Robert Hood, and Little John, together with their accomplices, whom the stupid populace openly celebrate wildly in comedies and tragedies and prefer to have them acted and sung above any other romances. In addition some commendable things are recited about him, as is shown here: Once when he was in Barnsdale on account of the king's wrath and the loud noises of the prince and was most devoutly hearing mass, as was his practice, he would not interrupt the service for any reason at all. One day when he was hearing mass, having been tracked down in that secluded woodland place by a certain sheriff and servants of the king, who had often threatened him before, some of his men realized what was happening, came to him and did their best to persuade him to flee. Because of his reverence for the sacrament, which he was then most devoutly venerating, he completely refused to do this. Although the rest of his men were trembling through fear of death, Robert, trusting only in him whom he revered in worship, together with the few men who happened to remain with him, attacked his enemies and easily overcame them. Made rich by the spoils he took from them and by their ransom, he singled out the servants of the church and the mass to be held in greater respect ever afterwards, bearing in mind what is commonly said: 'God listens to him who hears mass frequently.'

26 JOHN MAJOR

Historia Majoris Britanniae, tam Anglie quam Scotie, per Ioannem Maiorem, Nomine quidem Scotum, Professione autem Theologum, e Veterum Monumentis Concinnata
[Basle]: Jodocus Badius Ascensius, [1521].
5830

The *History of Greater Britain, both England and Scotland* by the Scottish historian John Major (1470-1550) is the first historical work to place Robin Hood's activity in the reign of Richard I. The passage in the text (fol. LV verso) reads in English translation:

Around these times, according to my conjecture, the English Robert Hood and Little John, celebrated robbers, lurked in the forests, plundering only wealthy men of their goods. They killed no one apart from those attacking or resisting them in the defence of their possessions. Robert maintained 100 archers most suited to fighting for these robberies, whom not even 400 of the bravest men dared to attack. The deeds of this Robert are enjoyed in songs all over Britain. He allowed no woman to be badly treated, nor did he pillage the goods of the poor; indeed, he nourished them lavishly with goods taken from abbots. I condemn the man's plundering, but of all robbers he was the most kind and the chief.

Major's words 'latronum omnium...princeps' are probably the ultimate source of Robin's reputation as 'prince of thieves'.

27 RICHARD GRAFTON

A Chronicle at Large and Meere History of the Affayres of Englande and Kinges of the Same...
London: Richard Tottle and Humpffrey Toye, 1569.
R1443

After quoting in English from John Major's account of Robin Hood, Grafton refers to different information he has from an old pamphlet, declaring Robin to be 'discended of a noble parentage: or rather beyng of a base stocke and linage, was for his manhoode and chiualry aduaunced to the noble dignitie of an Erle, excellyng principally in Archery'. As a result of falling into great debt he is outlawed and turns to robbery. Despite a price being put on his head, no man can catch him, and he is betrayed and bled to death at 'a certein Nonry in Yorkshire called Bircklies'. His gravestone bears the names of Robert Hood, William of Goldesborough and others.

Grafton also refers to the claim of Gerardus Mercator in his *Cosmography* that a town or village called Little Moravie in Scotland keeps the bones of a 'great and mightie man' called Little John.

28 WILLIAM CAMDEN

Britannia: or, a Chorographical Description of the Flourishing Kingdoms of England, Scotland, and Ireland, and the Islands Adjacent; from the Earliest Antiquity
Translated and enlarged by Richard Gough.
London: T. Payne and Son, and G.G.J. and J. Robinson, 1789.
R1757

A map of the south part of the West Riding of Yorkshire shows both Kirklees Hall and Robin Hood's Grave. In the text we find:

> *Kirklees* nunnery was founded t. Henry II. by Reyner of Flanders, for Cistercians, valued at £.19. *per annum.* In this house it is pretended Robin Hood was bled to death by design. His tomb with a plain cross on a flat stone is shewn in the cemetery. In the ground, at a little distance, lie two gravestones, one of which has the following inscription round a cross for one of the prioresses: Douce Jhu de fites (*or* eye) mercy a / Elizabeth de Staynton jadis priores de cest maison.

29 WILLIAM STUKELEY

Palaeographia Britannica: or, Discourses on Antiquities in Britain
Number II.
Stamford: printed by Francis Howgrave, 1746.
9048

The antiquary William Stukeley (1687-1765) made the most damaging contribution to studies on Robin Hood in the preposterous 'Pedigree of Robin Hood earl of Huntington' which he included in this volume. It is a work of misapplied learning with conjecture masquerading as fact.

30 [RICHARD GOUGH]

Sepulchral Monuments in Great Britain...
London: printed by J. Nichols, for the author, and sold by T. Payne and Son, 1786.
R1713

Gough comments as follows on Robin Hood's grave:

> *Kirklees* park, belonging to Sir George Armitage, bart. in the West Riding of Yorkshire. The figure of the stone over the grave of Robin Hood, now broken and much defaced, the inscription illegible. That printed in Thoresby, Ducat. Leod. 576, from Dr. Gale's papers, was never on it. The late Sir Samuel Armitage, owner of the premises, caused the ground under it to be dug a yard deep, and found it had never been disturbed; so that it was probably brought from some other place, and by vulgar tradition ascribed to Robin Hood.

6. Local Patriotism

31 SPENCER T. HALL
The Forester's Offering
London: Whitaker and Co., 1841.
Private collection

The author describes himself as 'a native of Sherwood Forest', and his book is an expression of local patriotism. Among the descriptions and poems that celebrate the Forest he places a section on the life of Robin Hood, largely based on the *Lytell Geste* and the early historians. He opts for the reign of Edward I as the period in which Robin lived. The frontispiece of the book depicts the Major Oak, reputed to be 500 years old and already a tourist attraction 150 years ago.

32 JOSEPH HUNTER
The Great Hero of the Ancient Minstrelsy of England, 'Robin Hood'. His Period, Real Character, etc. Investigated and Perhaps Ascertained
London: John Russell Smith, 1852.
Private collection

The historian Joseph Hunter (1783-1861) attempted to connect details of the *Lytell Geste* with archival evidence and thus 'prove' the historicity of Robin Hood. The poem's mention of 'Edward our comely king' is linked with the royal progress of Edward II through Yorkshire and Lancashire to Nottingham between April and November 1323. Hunter finds a Robyn or Robert Hood in royal service between March and November 1324, and he also traces a Robert Hood and wife Matilda in the court rolls of the manor of Wakefield in 1316 and 1317. These discrete 'facts' are pressed into service to form a biography. J.C. Holt provides a thorough critique of Hunter in *Robin Hood* (London: Thames and Hudson, revised edition, 1989) pp. 45-51.

33 J.W. WALKER
The True History of Robin Hood
With illustrations by Ethel W. Walker.
The West Yorkshire Printing Company Limited, 1952.
Private collection

This is another book rooting for the Wakefield Robert Hood. J.W. Walker parades his qualifications on the title-page – O.B.E., F.R.C.S., F.S.A., F.R.Hist.S. – but he treats the literary materials, whether early or later ballads or even Tennyson's *The Foresters*, without any sense that they embody historically different perceptions of Robin Hood.

34 P. VALENTINE HARRIS

The Truth about Robin Hood. A Refutation of the Mythologists' Theories, with New Evidence of the Hero's Actual Existence
Mansfield: Linney, 1978.
Private collection

A first version of this book was published in 1951. The author provides further occurrences of names from the *Gest* in archives of the early fourteenth century dealing with the Wakefield area. A firm believer in the historicity of Robin Hood, he pours scorn on the proponents of a mythological origin for Robin.

35 BRIAN LEWIS

Robin Hood a Yorkshire Man. The Case for the Wentbridge Robin Hood
Pontefract: Briton Press, 1994.
Private collection

This is a spirited polemic against Nottingham's commandeering of Robin Hood as its local hero: 'Nottinghamshire plays up its Robin Hood connection because as a county it has few natural assets... It is a county which has little to offer, except D.H. Lawrence...' Brian Lewis argues that the Nottingham of the ballads is a fictional name for the real local threat to the outlaws of Barnsdale, namely Pontefract.

Brian Lewis has also produced a portrait of Much the miller's son.

36 Publicity leaflet and summer timetable from 3 June 1996 for the Robin Hood Line
Private collection

The stretch of passenger railway line from Mansfield Woodhouse to Nottingham was opened in 1993 and is known as the Robin Hood Line.

7. Poems, Novels and Plays

37 *Keats*
Selected, arranged, and printed by T.J. Cobden-Sanderson.
Hammersmith: The Doves Press, 1914.
R38097

Keats's 'Robin Hood: To a Friend', written in 1818 in response to two poems from his friend J.R. Reynolds and first published in 1820, rejects his friend's nostalgia about Robin Hood, but does not quite escape it himself, although he notes the harsher aspects of the present.

The private presses of the late nineteenth and early twentieth centuries celebrated Keats's poetry. The John Rylands University Library of Manchester has editions by William Morris (Kelmscott Press, 1894) and Charles Ricketts (Ballantyne Press, London: Hacon & Ricketts, 1898) as well as Cobden-Sanderson. Nowhere else does Robin Hood receive such elegance of typographical design.

38 [WALTER SCOTT]
Historical Romances of the Author of Waverley
2 vols.
Vol. 1. *Ivanhoe.*
Edinburgh: Archibald Constable and Co.; London: Hurst, Robinson and Co., 1822.
R18437.13/43

Scott's *Ivanhoe* was first published at the end of 1819 in an edition dated 1820. Into this novel of hostilities between the Normans and the descendants of the Saxons Scott introduces as minor figures Robin Hood, Friar Tuck (as the Clerk of Copmanhurst) and others of his merry men. Although replete with historical inaccuracies, *Ivanhoe* has remained one of Scott's most popular and vital novels. The edition shown here is heavily grangerized, i.e. it is filled with a mass of illustrations taken from other publications and inserted at a later date.

39 PIERCE EGAN
Robin Hood and Little John or the Merry Men of Sherwood Forest
Illustrated by W.H. Thwaites.
London: W.S. Johnson & Co., 1850.
Private collection

Pierce Egan the younger (1814-80) was one of the leading writers of popular literature for the Victorian working classes. His *Robin Hood* was first published in 1839-40 in forty-one parts at a penny each. The traditional material is refashioned to suit the tastes of a readership that revelled in the clichés of sentimental love, adventures involving physical violence and last-minute escapes, all told at copious length. Robin, the dispossessed heir to the earldom of Huntingdon, is brought as a baby to Gilbert and Margaret Head in Sherwood. His chief opponent in later life is Baron Fitz Alwine of Nottingham, whose daughter, Christabel, marries Allan Clare (Allen a Dale of the ballads). Allan Clare's sister is Marian, who is married to Robin Hood. Egan makes use of details from *Ivanhoe* and makes a nod at the great ballad editor by naming Margaret Head's brother Roland Ritson. The novel was republished many times up to the end of the century.

40 ALFRED LORD TENNYSON
The Foresters. Robin Hood and Maid Marian
London and New York: Macmillan and Co., 1892.
Private collection

This play by Tennyson (1809-92), written in a mixture of prose and blank verse, makes Maid Marian the daughter of Sir Richard Lea, in love with Robin Hood, the outlawed Earl of Huntingdon, but wooed by both the Sheriff of Nottingham and Prince John. In escaping to the greenwood, Marian's relationship with Robin remains chaste, but she becomes Queen of the Woods.

41 ALFRED NOYES
Collected Poems
Fifth impression.
Vol. 1.
Edinburgh and London: William Blackwood & Sons, 1914.
R38085

Noyes's poem 'Sherwood', first published in 1904, embodies a sentimental longing for a rural 'merry England' where Robin's 'merry thieves' and 'robber band' do nothing more dangerous than 'go by'.

42 ALFRED NOYES
Robin Hood
A play in five acts.
London: William Blackwood & Sons Ltd, 1926.
R71586

This play by Alfred Noyes (1880-1958) was first published in an earlier version in New York in 1911, but did not appear in Britain until 1926. The greenwood setting requires forest sprites and a fool called Shadow-of-a-leaf. It ends with Elinor, the sister of Princes Richard and John, killing both Robin Hood and Maid Marian. In Act II Friar Tuck enunciates the 'golden rules' of the democratic company that defend the poor and respect all womankind.

43 NICHOLAS CHASE
Locksley
London: Heinemann, 1983.
Private collection

The hero of this novel, Robert Atheling, Earl of Locksley, tells his story in the first person, moving from Sicily and the crusade of Richard the Lionheart, through various parts of England and France. Locksley adopts the persona of Robin Hood, but Marian is his sister rather than his forest bride, and her first love is the Frenchman Jean Neuilly, who plays the role of Little John. The tale is one of political intrigue and brutality, ending with the loss of the crown jewels and the death of King John. This is emphatically not a greenwood idyll, but reflects the harshness of life under the dominion of a tyrant.

8. Nineteenth-Century Children's Books

44 BARBARA HOFLAND
Theodore, or the Crusader. A Tale for Youth
London: John Harris and Son, [1821].
Private collection

The youthful crusader Theodore, setting off on the Third Crusade in the company of Richard Coeur de Lion (Richard I), has a brief encounter with Robin Hood, disguised as St Grimbald, in a cavern near Knaresborough. Robin has come there from Sherwood and declares that he will one day become Earl of Huntingdon. Barbara Hofland (1770-1844) was the author of many moral and historical tales for children.

45 STEPHEN PERCY
[pseudonym of **JOSEPH CUNDALL**]
Robin Hood and his Merry Foresters
Third edition.
Westminster: Joseph Cundall, 1845.
Private collection

The first edition of this book was published by Tilt and Bogue in 1841. It is an early retelling in prose of the Robin Hood stories for children. The eight illustrations are lithographs of designs by John Gilbert.

46 *The Celebrated History of the Renowned Robin Hood, the Merry Outlaw of Sherwood Forest. To which is Added, The Professor of Signs*
Glasgow: printed for the Booksellers, *c.* 1830-40.
Private collection

This twenty-four-page chapbook presents a condensed account of Robin's adventures, set in Sherwood Forest and Nottingham in the time of Richard I.

47 *History of Robin Hood*
Penny Pictorial Library.
Otley: Yorkshire Joint Stock Publishing and Stationery Company, Limited, *c.* 1855.
Private collection

This twelve-page chapbook contains a text with some similarities to, and some differences from, the Glasgow chapbook. Its main formal difference lies in its eight illustrations, of which the first has been crudely hand-coloured, a task that at this period was often performed by children.

48 *Robin Hood and his Merry Men*
Aunt Louisa's London Toy Books.
London: Frederick Warne & Co., *c.* 1867.
Private collection

'Aunt Louisa' was the pseudonym of Mrs Laura Valentine, the general editor at Frederick Warne & Co. The artist who illustrated these well-known episodes is nowhere named. Toy books were a form of large picture book with colour-printed pictures and a small amount of text that started to be produced in the 1850s. It is worth noting that one of the episodes focuses on Maid Marian.

49 JOHN B. MARSH
The Life and Adventures of Robin Hood
London and New York: George Routledge and Sons, *c.* 1865.
Private collection

This version of the Robin Hood stories combines incidents from the old ballads with the author's invention to make a long adventure book. Its topographical focus is Sherwood and Nottingham, with only the death scene at Kirklees in Yorkshire. The six colour-plates are unattributed. The book proved popular, and there are at least eight editions up to the First World War.

50 WILLIAM HEATON
The Story of Robin Hood
With illustrations printed in colours.
Third edition.
London and New York: Cassell, Petter and Galpin, *c.* 1878.
Private collection

This retelling of the old ballads avoids fictional amplification and makes no mention of Maid Marian. Indeed, in his faithfulness to the ballads the author is constrained to make explanatory comments and corrections, so that his book is a mixture of narrative and historical analysis. His Robin is born at Lockesley in Yorkshire or, he says, 'as some recent writers think, in Warwickshire' about 1160. The episodes flit between Nottinghamshire and Yorkshire. The eight lively colour-plates are unattributed.

9. Comparable Heroes

51 *The Mad Pranks and Merry Jests of Robin Goodfellow*
Reprinted from the edition of 1628.
With an introduction by J. Payne Collier.
London: The Percy Society, 1841.
R984.2/32

Robin Goodfellow is the offspring of the King of the Fairies and a human mother. He has been linked with Robin Hood by those who look for a supernatural rather than a historical origin for the greenwood hero. Robin Goodfellow is a trickster figure, and some of his pranks are uncommonly like those of the German Till Eulenspiegel. However, the chapter describing 'How Robin Goodfellow helped two lovers and deceived an old man' shows a similarity to the ballad of *Robin Hood and Allen a Dale*.

52 AMY CRUSE
The Book of Epic Heroes
With eighty-four illustrations in colour and black and white.
London, Calcutta, Sydney: George G. Harrap & Company Ltd, 1926.
Private collection

Hereward the Wake is mentioned in the *Anglo-Saxon Chronicle*, and his life was recorded in Latin in the early twelfth century. He led resistance to the Norman conquerors about 1070 in south Lincolnshire and the Fens. Modern awareness of his exploits owes much to Charles Kingsley's novel, first published in 1866. He frequently figures in children's books about historical and legendary heroes and is included by Amy Cruse alongside heroes such as Odysseus, Beowulf, Robin Hood and William Tell.

53 *The History of William Tell, the Swiss Patriot; the Saviour of his Country*
With a frontispiece.
London: W.S. Johnson, *c.* 1839.
Private collection

The story of William Tell is linked with the struggle for Swiss independence in the early fourteenth century. He is a more political figure than Robin Hood, but his historicity has been strongly questioned. The episode in which he is forced to shoot an apple placed on his small son's head uses a motif found in many other sources, including the ballad of *Adam Bell, Clim of the Clough, and William of Cloudesly*. This particular English book is an adaptation and abridgement of Barbara Hofland's translation of Jean Pierre Claris de Florian's *Guillaume Tell* (1802).

54 *Adam Bell, Clym of the Cloughe, and Wyllyam of Cloudesle*
In: *Pieces of Ancient Popular Poetry: from Authentic Manuscripts and Old Printed Copies*
Edited by Joseph Ritson.
London: T. and J. Egerton, 1791.
7473

This late medieval ballad of three outlaws from the Forest of Inglewood, between Carlisle and Penrith, survives in various sixteenth-century prints and enjoyed considerable popularity up to the end of the seventeenth century. William of Cloudesly is betrayed by an old woman and captured in Carlisle; he is rescued by his two fellow outlaws and finally demonstrates his skill in archery by shooting an apple on his son's head. This feat is best known in connection with the Swiss popular hero, William Tell, but it crops up in several other sources too.

55 *Walt Disney's Rob Roy the Highland Rogue*
The Walt Disney motion picture version of *The Adventures of Rob Roy the Highland Rogue*.
Based upon the screen play by Lawrence Edward Watkin and adapted by Edward Boyd.
London and Glasgow: William Collins Sons and Co. Ltd, 1954.
Private collection

Scotland's counterpart to Robin Hood is the drover, outlaw and cattle-thief Rob Roy MacGregor, who had his base near Aberfoyle, Tayside, and died in 1734. He was immortalized by Sir Walter Scott in his novel *Rob Roy* (1817). The Disney film, like many another, puts historical veracity way below the claims of visually exciting adventure.

56 W. HARRISON AINSWORTH
Jack Sheppard. A Romance
With illustrations by George Cruikshank.
London: Richard Bentley, 1839.
14689

Popular fascination with the lives of highwaymen and pirates goes back at least to the early eighteenth century, and Robin Hood was often included among them. Harrison Ainsworth (1805-82) mined this rich seam, romanticizing Dick Turpin in *Rookwood* (1834) and dealing with Jack Sheppard and Jonathan Wild in the volume displayed here. Both Ainsworth and his illustrator Cruikshank revelled in the horrors and hair's-breadth escapes of these stories.

57 *Dick Turpin's Daring Disguise*
Newnes' 'Black Bess' Library, no. 30.
6 May 1922.
Private collection

The most famous of all English highwaymen, Dick Turpin (1705-39) has had all manner of exploits attributed to him in fiction. This weekly series of magazines devoted to his adventures was produced by George Newnes, price 2*d*. Black Bess was Turpin's horse, on whom he is supposed to have galloped from London to York on one desperate overnight ride.

58 GEORGE BORROW
Wild Wales. Its People, Language, and Scenery
London: John Murray, 1919.
R47155

Borrow's *Wild Wales*, first published in 1862, relates several of the exploits of the man known as the Welsh Robin Hood in connection with his visit to Tregaron, where he was born. This is Twm Shon Catty, one Thomas Jones, the son of Catherine or Catty, who was born at the end of the sixteenth century and became a clever thief. He was more of a trickster than an adventurer, married a fine lady and eventually became a justice of the peace.

59 *Schinderhannes. Kriminalgeschichte voller Abentheuer und Wunder und doch streng der Wahrheit getreu. 1802*
Wiederaufgefunden, herausgegeben, mit Dokumenten und Bildern versehen von Manfred Franke.
Berlin: Verlag Klaus Wagenbach, 1977.
Private collection

Germany's most famous criminal adventurer is Johannes Bückler (1783-1803), generally known as Schinderhannes ('Knacker Jack'). He began his career of robbery and murder at the age of fourteen and was executed at the age of twenty. His notoriety spread far enough for the Scottish writer Leitch Ritchie to compose a novel entitled *Schinderhannes, the Robber of the Rhine* (London and Belfast: Simms and M'Intyre, 1848).

10. Maid Marian

60 ADAM DE LA HALLE
Li Gieus de Robin et de Marion
In: *Théâtre Français au Moyen-Âge*, publié d'après les manuscrits de la Bibliothèque du Roi par MM. L.J.N. Monmerqué et Francisque Michel.
Paris: H. Delloye editeur et Firmin Didot Frères imprimeurs-libraires, 1839.
R46406

This medieval French play, written *c.* 1280, derives from the lyric tradition of the *pastourelle*, in which a shepherdess is approached by a knight to be his lover, with a variety of possible outcomes. Here the shepherdess is called Marion, her peasant lover Robin. With the help of his friends, Robin repels the knight, and general festivities take place. Some such tradition seems to lie behind the English May games and plays of the fifteenth and sixteenth centuries in which Marian appears as Robin Hood's partner.

61 BEN JONSON
The Sad Shepherd: or, a Tale of Robin Hood, a Fragment
With a continuation, notes, and an appendix.
London: J. Nichols, 1783.
Private collection

Only a little more than two acts were completed of Jonson's play, first published in 1641. This pastoral drama tells of the troubled love of the sad shepherd Aeglamour and the beautiful shepherdess Earine, with which are intertwined the troubles of Robin Hood and his mistress, Maid Marian, who is a fine huntress. The cause of their troubles is Maudlin, the

This is an unabridged and unaltered republication of a book first published in New York by Charles Scribner's Sons in 1883. Howard Pyle (1853-1911) was one of the great American illustrators of the nineteenth century, and his *Robin Hood* has lasted well despite his mixture of verbal archaisms and simple, direct language. The book is a celebration of male camaraderie – Maid Marian is only fleetingly mentioned – and merry England or, rather, merry Nottinghamshire.

68 EVA MARCH TAPPAN

Robin Hood: his Book
Illustrated by Charlotte Harding.
Boston: Little, Brown, and Company, 1912.
Private collection

This is a series of episodes rather than a connected biography of Robin Hood. It has a fanciful fairytale about his birth and ends with his marriage to Marian. Robin is an outlaw 'not for crime as we count crime, but for shooting the king's deer'. One innovation is the use of the little old woman who provides Robin with a disguise to escape the bishop's men as a figure linking other episodes. For an English reader the book has some oddities, such as imagining Bernisdale (not Barnsdale) as a town. The book was first published in 1903.

69 ELINOR M. BUCKINGHAM

The Tale of Robin Hood and his Merry Men
In: *Children's Own Library*, edited by J. Ellis Burdick with a general introduction by Charles Welsh. Vol. 5, *Legendary Stories.*
New York: National Library Company, 1910.
Private collection

Elinor Buckingham places her Robin Hood in the period of King Edward, although the editor's introductory note seems to prefer his being born about 1160. Buckingham includes the story of Gamelyn as giving the history of Will Scarlet (in other versions he starts as Gamwell and is Robin's nephew), but she generally keeps close to the ballad stories. The illustrations seem to have been taken from several different sources; the artists are not identified.

70 TILMAN RÖHRIG

Robin Hood: solang es Unrecht gibt
Hamburg: Cecilie Dressler Verlag, 1994.
Private collection

German scholarly interest in Robin Hood goes back to the nineteenth century, but there have been various independent German children's books since the Second World War. Tilman Röhrig (1945-) did research in libraries and on the ground before writing his grippingly realistic novel. Like Scott in *Ivanhoe* and Nicholas Chase in *Locksley*, he introduces a positively-depicted Jewish character. His Marian is not Robin's eventual bride, but a girl who is brutally orphaned and treated as a daughter by Little John, whose personality is strongly developed. The second part of the title means 'as long as there is injustice'.

12. Early Twentieth-Century Children's Books

71 *The Noble Birth and Gallant Atchievements of that Remarkable Outlaw Robin Hood Together with a True Account of the Many Merry & Extravagant Exploits he Play'd*
In twelve several stories: newly collected into one volume: by an ingenious antiquary.
Early English Prose Romances, part II.
Edited by W.J. Thoms.
[Illustrated by Harold Nelson.]
Edinburgh: Otto Schulze & Co., 1903.
Private collection

The text was originally printed in London for Thomas Vere and William Gilbertson in 1662. Thoms's edition was first published in 1828. The illustrator of the 1903 edition, Harold Nelson (1871-1946), was a great admirer of Dürer.

72 HENRY GILBERT
Robin Hood and the Men of the Greenwood
With sixteen illustrations in colour by Walter Crane.
Edinburgh and London: T.C. and E.C. Jack, [1912].
Private collection

Henry Gilbert's version of the Robin Hood stories was reprinted several times up to the 1950s, and an abridged version was issued in 1915. Based on 'the best episodes related in the ballads', it also contains much invented material, including a Norman castle at Wrangby called Evil Hold and a multiplicity of Norman lords. The sixteen colour-plates by Walter Crane (1845-1915) are a far cry from his vibrant early work and represent, in Isobel Spencer's words, a 'capitulation to pictorial illusionism'.

73 *Robin Hood and his Merry Outlaws*
Retold by F.C. Tilney.
With coloured illustrations by Ione Railton.
London: J.M. Dent Limited; New York: E.P. Dutton & Company, [1913].
Private collection

The twenty-two chapters present a prose 'paraphrase of the finest and most rational ballads in the Robin Hood cycle'. Maid Marian is included. Tilney, following Hunter, opts for the reign of Edward II as the historical setting. The illustrator, Ione Railton, is probably a relative of the better-known Herbert Railton (1858-1910).

74 ROSE YEATMAN WOOLF
Robin Hood and his Life in the Merry Greenwood
Illustrated by Howard Davie and edited by Capt. [Edric] Vredenburg.
London, Paris, New York: Raphael Tuck & Sons Ltd, *c.* 1919.
Private collection

This traditional outline of Robin's deeds in the period of King Richard I gives plenty of space to his relationship with Lady Marian as well as his usual exploits. It is copiously illustrated in black and white with eight colour-plates by Howard Davie (fl. 1914-35), who seems to have worked only for Raphael Tuck. The book concludes with Robin's death and the following final paragraph:

> The heritage he has left us manifests itself to-day when Englishmen rise in their millions to defend the weak and oppressed of other lands, crushed beneath the heel of a cruel and ruthless invader. It will be ours whilst we continue to cry in love and loyalty, as did Robin Hood nigh seven hundred years ago – 'God save Merrie England and our King'.

75 J. WALKER McSPADDEN AND CHARLES WILSON
Robin Hood and his Merry Outlaws
With eight colour-plates by N.C. Wyeth.
London, Bombay, Sydney: George G. Harrap & Co. Ltd, first published September 1921, reprinted April 1932.
Private collection

This retelling of the traditional tales is accompanied by some of the most attractive illustrations from the early twentieth century by the American artist Newell Convers Wyeth (1882-1945).

76 E. CHARLES VIVIAN
Robin Hood and his Merry Men
With forty-eight colour-plates by Harry G. Theaker.
London and Melbourne: Ward, Lock & Co., Limited, *c.* 1930.
Private collection

While Gilbert's book opens with high summer, Vivian's begins in the depths of winter. Otherwise they have much in common, including the Norman lords and Evil Hold. Harry G. Theaker (1873-1954), who was Principal of the Regent Street Polytechnic School of Art from 1931 to 1938, was a prolific illustrator. His designs for *Robin Hood* are varied in format and style, some even taking on that of a comic cartoon.

13. Noted Children's Authors

77 GEOFFREY TREASE
Bows Against the Barons
With illustrations by Jack Matthew.
New edition.
London: Lawrence & Wishart, 1948.
Private collection

This Marxist interpretation of the figure of Robin Hood was first published in 1934. Its central figure is a boy called Dickon, who becomes involved with Robin and his companions in their struggle against Sir Rolf of D'Eyncourt Castle. Robin says: 'If we all stand together we can beat D'Eyncourt. Some day we can clear England of masters from sea to sea'. The historical background is left general without names of kings or specific crusades.

78 CAROLA OMAN
Robin Hood, the Prince of Outlaws. A Tale of the Fourteenth Century from the 'Lytell Geste'
Illustrated with line-drawings and eight colour-plates by S. van Abbé.
London: J.M. Dent & Sons Ltd; New York: E.P. Dutton & Co. Inc., 1954.
Private collection

First published in 1939, Carola Oman's version locates the exploits of Robin Hood in the period of Edward II. She follows several of the old ballads and groups them under four headings – 'Robin Hood and Sir Richard', 'The Sheriff of Nottingham', 'Robin Hood and his Merry Men' and 'Robin, Marian, and the King'. The illustrations are by Salomon van Abbé (1883-1955), who was born in Amsterdam, but came to England at the age of five and later became a British citizen. The illustration depicts the capture of Sir Richard at the Lee in Barnesdale.

79 ENID BLYTON
Tales of Brave Adventure
London: Dean & Son Ltd, 1963.
Private collection

This book by Enid Blyton (1897-1968) consists of a reprint of her earlier *Robin Hood Book* (London: Latimer House, 1949) together with stories about King Arthur and his knights. She had also written two Robin Hood plays (1927 and 1935) as well as a *Tales of Robin Hood* (1930). The stories in the book displayed are characteristically simplified forms of the most popular ballads, rather unusually including 'Robin Hood and the Tinker of Banbury'.

80 ROSEMARY SUTCLIFF
The Chronicles of Robin Hood
Illustrated by C. Walter Hodges.
London: Geoffrey Cumberlege, Oxford University Press, 1950.
Private collection

Rosemary Sutcliff (1920-92) was the author of many distinguished children's books with historical, legendary and mythological themes. *The Chronicles of Robin Hood* was her first published book, based largely on the best-known ballads. C. Walter Hodges (1909-) was a prolific illustrator and also wrote many books himself.

81 ANTONIA PAKENHAM
Robin Hood
Illustrated by Geoffrey Whittam.
London: The Heirloom Library, 1955.
Private collection

Another product of the 1950s, Antonia Pakenham's *Robin Hood* features a Norman baron implausibly bearing the Saxon forename Oswald, and a treacherous friend of Maid Marian called Black Barbara. A boy called Dickon Barleycorn appears on the opening pages. Geoffrey Whittam (1916-) illustrated a large number of children's books from the 1950s onwards.

82 ANTONIA FRASER
Robin Hood
Illustrated by Rebecca Fraser.
London: Sidgwick & Jackson, 1971.
Private collection

This is a re-issue of Antonia Pakenham's *Robin Hood,* illustrated by her daughter Rebecca Fraser.

83 *The Adventures of Robin Hood*
Collected and retold by Roger Lancelyn Green.
Illustrated by Arthur Hall.
Puffin Books, PS 101.
Harmondsworth: Penguin Books, 1960.
Private collection

First published in 1956, this collection of adventures is based firmly on the old ballads, but adds material from Robert Greene, Ben Jonson, Scott's *Ivanhoe* and elsewhere. It has been reprinted many times. Arthur Hall (1906-83) was Head of the School of Graphic Design at Kingston School of Art from 1952 to 1974.

14. Robin Hood in Performance

84 ENID BLYTON
The Play's the Thing! Musical Plays for Children
With music by Alec Rowley and twenty-four full-page drawings by Alfred E. Bestall.
London: The Home Library Book Company (George Newnes Ltd), [1927].
Private collection

The last play in the collection is a four-act piece called 'Merry Robin Hood' which presents the contest for the silver arrow. Alfred E. Bestall became better known from 1935 to 1965 as illustrator of the Rupert books, taking over from Mary Tourtel when her eyesight failed.

85 *The Adventures of Robin Hood*
With sixteen plates in colour, 100 illustrations and text based on the First National Pictures' Technicolor production of 'The Adventures of Robin Hood'.
London and Melbourne: Ward, Lock & Co. Limited, *c.* 1938.
Private collection

The American film of 1938 was directed by Michael Curtiz and William Keighley, with Errol Flynn and Olivia de Havilland. It was the seventh Robin Hood film to be made.

86 *Walt Disney's Story of Robin Hood and his Merrie Men*
Based upon the screen play by Laurence Edward Watkin and adapted by Edward Boyd.
London and Glasgow: Collins, 1952.
Private collection

This film, directed by Ken Annakin, starred Richard Todd as Robin and Joan Rice as Marian.

87 *Robin and the Greenwood Gang: a Cantata-Musical for Piano, Bass and Drums or any Suitable Combination of Instruments*
Music by Philip Lane. Lyrics by Philippa Frischmann and Philip Lane.
London: Universal Edition, 1981.
Private collection

Fifteen songs present the kernel of the traditional Robin Hood story in a lively, humorous style. In the first song it is said of Prince John 'He robs the poor to pay the rich', reversing what is more commonly asserted about Robin. During Margaret Thatcher's premiership it was frequently claimed that she did the same as Prince John and was the reverse of Robin Hood.

88 DAVID NEILSON
Robin Hood – the Truth Behind the Green Tights. A Play
London, New York, Sydney, Toronto, Hollywood: Samuel French, 1984.
Private collection

This pantomime play, crammed with corny jokes and topical satire, typifies one prominent trend of the late twentieth century – turning the traditional Robin Hood story into the subject of comedy, 'sending it up'. The plot focuses on the Sheriff of Nottingham's attempt to marry his niece, Maid Marian, to Sir Guy of Gisbourne. Will Scarlet appears in the guise of Will Scargill (an allusion to the miners' leader, Arthur Scargill). There is also a passing reference to Mark the Thatcher's son, whom the Sheriff condemns to 'seven days in the stocks and a course in map-reading'. (Mark Thatcher, the Prime Minister's son, had recently lost his way in the Sahara Desert.)

89 ANTHONY HOROWITZ
Richard Carpenter's Robin of Sherwood: the Hooded Man
Harmondsworth: Puffin Books, 1986.
Private collection

This is the book of one of the HTV series *Robin of Sherwood* that ran from 1984 to 1986. Michael Praed had left at the end of the second series, so his place, now as the dispossessed Earl of Huntingdon, was taken by Jason Connery. Judi Trott played Marian. This series took Robin's adventures into the realms of magic, the occult and paganism, introducing the figure of Herne the Hunter as a supernatural power giving strength to Robin, while at the same time leading figures of the Church are portrayed as sinister and corrupt. The fight between good and evil focuses on a sword called Albion. The Saracen Nasir, who has returned with Richard from the crusade, is a valued member of Robin's company.

90 GARTH PEARCE
Robin Hood: Prince of Thieves. The Official Movie Book
London: Hamlyn, 1991.
Private collection

This film of Robin Hood, with Kevin Costner in the title role, begins with him on the crusade in the Holy Land. There he saves the life of the Black Saracen Azeem, who accompanies him to England and becomes his right-hand man. Mary Elizabeth Mastrantonio plays a rather Pre-Raphaelite Maid Marian, but the most striking character is Alan Rickman as the villainous Sheriff of Nottingham, a devotee of black magic with the witch Mortianna, played by Geraldine McEwan. Sean Connery puts in an appearance at the end as Richard the Lionheart, much more grizzled and old than the real Richard was.

91 Publicity leaflet for *Robin Prince of Sherwood,* playing at the Palace Theatre, Manchester, 29 June-3 July 1994
Private collection

This musical, created by the production team of *Joseph and the Amazing Technicolor Dreamcoat,* was brought from London's West End and also went to several other provincial venues. The critic of the *Guardian* liked 'its energy, its fun, its clever lyrics and ability to mix plaintive moments...with self-parody', but he also thought the story-line 'pretty feeble'.

100 *Robin Hood and his Merry Men*
Pictures and rhymes by Trelleck.
London: Raphael Tuck, 1945.
Private collection

A colourfully-illustrated modern verse retelling for young readers of eight tales of Robin Hood, including many of the best-known stories.

101 MAX KESTER
The Silver Arrow. A Robin Hood Adventure
Illustrated by John Kenney.
Loughborough: Wills & Hepworth Ltd, *c.* 1954.
Private collection

This story, originally written for broadcasting in 1940 in a different form, includes the episode in which Robin shoots his arrow and splits a willow wand in two. This example of a 'Ladybird' book was designed for children of eight years of age or younger.

102 *Legends of Man*
Reading 360. The Ginn Reading Programme. Level 13. Book 1.
Aylesbury: Ginn and Company Ltd, third impression, 1980.
Private collection

Along with retellings of famous tales from around the world, such as those of Odysseus, Beowulf, *The Man from Ironbark* and the Cid, this reader gives an account of Robin Hood and his merry men by the American writer Louis Untermeyer.

103 *Learning English. Red Line 2*
Unterrichtswerk für Realschulen.
Herausgegeben von Stuart Amor, Rosemary Hellyer-Jones, Peter Lampater, Helmut Reisener und Rolf W. Roth sowie Werner Beile und Alice Beile-Bowes.
Stuttgart: Ernst Klett Schulbuchverlag, 1996.
Private collection

This German textbook for thirteen-year-olds includes a dozen pages devoted to Nottingham and Robin Hood. In 'Robin Hood and the black cloak' it presents a simplified version of the rescue of Will Scarlet from the gallows.

17. Recent Highlights in Children's Versions

104 *Robin Hood*
Adapted from the version by Alexandre Dumas.
Illustrated by Benvenuti.
London: W.H. Allen and Co. Ltd, *c.* 1961.
Private collection

This is no. 15 in a large-size, copiously illustrated series called Splendour Books, which includes such other classics as *Pinocchio* and *The Arabian Nights*. The illustrations, modelled stylistically on late medieval manuscripts, are more decorative than emotionally evocative.

105 BERNARD MILES
Robin Hood. His Life and Legend
Illustrated by Victor G. Ambrus.
London, New York, Sydney, Toronto: Hamlyn, 1979.
Private collection

Bernard Miles has Robin Hood and his boyhood friend Marian hail from Hartoft, a village in north-east Yorkshire. He also invents winter quarters for the outlaws in a cave near Bolsover that has now mysteriously been engulfed in the sinking of a coal-shaft. His retelling of the tales is a heady mixture of tradition, historical description and imagination. The illustrations of Victor Ambrus (1930-) are boldly evocative.

106 *Robin Hood*
Retold by Sarah Hayes.
Illustrated by Patrick Benson.
London: Walker Books, 1989.
Private collection

Sarah Hayes's Robin will not kill a hind with a fawn or an unarmed man and has as his maxim 'rob the rich to feed the poor'. This crisply narrated selection of his deeds is illustrated by extraordinarily striking black-and-white scraperboard pictures by Patrick Benson.

107 MICHAEL MORPURGO
Robin of Sherwood
Illustrated by Michael Foreman.
Published in association with The National Trust.
London: Pavilion Books Limited, 1996.
Private collection

This up-to-date reworking of the life of Robin Hood comes in the form of a dream that a boy has when his favourite tree is blown down in a hurricane. Robin has a father who is blinded by Guy of Gisbourne, he marries Marion, and they have a son called Martin. Marion is an albino, part of the group of Outcasts in the forest, whom Robin joins and whose leader he becomes. Their exploits include journeying to Austria to ransom and rescue Richard the

Lionheart. At the end of the story the Abbess of Kirkleigh poisons not only Robin but also Little John and Friar Tuck. Much the miller's son brings the news to Marion, who wants only to remember Robin from when he was alive. This reverberant, subtly written book is evocatively illustrated by Michael Foreman.

108 *The Adventures of Robin Hood*
Retold and illustrated by Marcia Williams.
London, Boston, Sydney: Walker Books and associates, 1996.
Private collection

Cartoon-style retellings of the traditional stories exist from at least the middle of the twentieth century, but this version differs in its rollicking comedy. It is a good example of our own period's embarrassment with regard to traditional tales and legends. They are constantly guyed rather than told 'straight'. But even this is a homage to the lasting power of the material. In this version the Prioress of Kirklees claims to be a kinswoman of Sir Guy of Gisborne.

18. An Old Hero Ever New

109 PARKE GODWIN
Sherwood
New York: Avon Books, 1992.
Private collection

PARKE GODWIN
Robin and the King
New York: Avon Books, 1994.
Private collection

These two action-packed novels, first published in 1991 and 1993 respectively, are the compliment of a late twentieth-century American popular novelist to Scott. He keeps to a Robin Hood in the context of conflict between Normans and Saxons, but places events in the immediate aftermath of the Norman invasion. Occasional traditional episodes are subsumed in a detailed historical picture which includes the rescue of a precious manuscript of the *Anglo-Saxon Chronicle* and its transportation to Abingdon. Godwin is passionately interested in making his characters rounded and psychologically plausible, whether it is the Conqueror or his son Rossel (Rufus) in the sequel *Robin and the King* or Robin and the other characters. Robin Hood is the nickname of the Saxon thane Edward of Denby, married to a down-to-earth, sensual Marian. She is only one of several strongly painted women – Robin's mother Maud, imprisoned but indomitable; his cousin Judith, married to Ralf Fitz-Gerald, Sheriff of Nottingham; William's diminutive, shrewd queen Matilda. Will Scarlet is Robin's Welsh serf Will Scatloch, Little John the village blacksmith John Littlerede and something of a rival. But Godwin is much more interested in exploring the complex and subtle relationship between Robin and Ralf Fitz-Gerald, which he does not see in the black-and-white terms of the old ballads. Indeed, Godwin largely parts company from the ballads and their simple oppositions, but creates a Robin fit for our own times.

110 STEVE WILSON
Robin Hood: the Spirit of the Forest
London: Neptune Press, 1993.
Private collection

This book is representative of current interest in paganism, comparative mythology, nature worship and 'green' issues. Historic and literary aspects of Robin Hood fade into insignificance as the mythological context becomes even more important than Robin himself. The author describes himself as 'a priest in the *Fellowship of Isis*'.

111 JOHN MATTHEWS
Robin Hood: Green Lord of the Wildwood
Foreword by Richard Carpenter. Afterword by Chesca Potter.
Glastonbury: Gothic Image Publications, 1993.
Private collection

John Matthews has written prolifically in the fields of Celtic and Arthurian mythology and native spirituality, and his book has more scholarly substance than Steve Wilson's. His Robin Hood belongs to folklore and the religion of nature, being linked especially to the figure of the Green Man. The book includes two 'masques' – *The Masque of the Wildwood* and *The Challenge of the Green Knight* – which give expression to these values.

112 *The Story of Robin Hood: from the First Minstrel Tellings, Ballads and May Games*
Retold by Robert Leeson.
Illustrated by Barbara Lofthouse.
London: Kingfisher, 1994.
Private collection

This brightly-illustrated retelling of a selection of the old ballads avoids placing Robin in a specific period of the Middle Ages. The king is unnamed and Robin is described as a yeoman outlaw, but also as 'King of the Summer, Lord of the Greenwood and the Prince of Thieves'.

113 NEIL PHILIP
Robin Hood
Illustrated by Nick Harris.
London, New York, Stuttgart, Moscow: Dorling Kindersley, 1997.
Private collection

This is a carefully packaged book. The publisher's blurb states it to be based on the medieval ballads but it makes Robin into the Earl of Huntingdon and Maid Marian into Marian Fitzwalter. When he dies at Kirklees it is in Marian's arms, not those of Little John. In addition to providing a story, the book is a primer of medieval history, packed with information and pictures on every page, using images from medieval manuscripts, historical artefacts and photographs. Instruction is very skilfully integrated into what is usually straightforward narration.